How Fiction Works

Additional Praise for *How Fiction Works*

An *Economist* Best Book of the Year
A *Kansas City Star* Best Book of the Year
A *Library Journal* Best Book of the Year
A *San Francisco Chronicle* Top 50 Best
Nonfiction Book of the Year

"An articulate reminder of the framework that is essential to constructing a lasting work of the imagination."   —*The Miami Herald*

"Wood's arranging of source material to prove his points is as fluid and lovely as any great composer's arrangement of musical notes, and, if nothing else, *How Fiction Works* will inspire you to simply read more. . . . [A] lovely, eloquent ode to reading."   —*The Oregonian*

"This admirable book is, among other things, a successful attempt to replace E. M. Forster's *Aspects of the Novel* as an accessible guide to the mechanics of fiction. Without losing sight of its promise to address the common reader rather than the specialist, *How Fiction Works* is much more sophisticated than Forster's book. . . . Wood has thought keenly and profitably about such matters. He also benefits, as Forster did not, from wide reading in contemporary fiction."   —Frank Kermode, *The New Republic*

"A perceptive and graceful essay, which almost anybody who's interested in books could read. . . . Well worth reading."

—*The Sunday Independent* (UK)

"Highly stimulating stuff—if it doesn't make you hug your bookcase gratefully, you're probably an incorrigible 'formalist-cum-structuralist.'"

—*Kirkus Reviews*

"Through Wood's close, mostly loving, frequently funny, occasionally dizzying examination, our reading experience is amplified and enriched. . . . Wood's wit and occasional hilarious commentary are well timed and sizzlingly accurate."

—*Virginia Quarterly Review*

"By examining the minutiae of character, narrative, and style in a range of fictional works that starts with the Bible and ends with Coetzee and Pynchon, he fondly and delicately pieces back together what the deconstructors put asunder."

—*The Guardian* (UK)

"Serious readers of fiction will tackle this informing and enlightening new work with unrestrained relish."

—*Library Journal*

ALSO BY JAMES WOOD

How Fiction Works

Tenth Anniversary Edition

Updated and Expanded

JAMES WOOD

❧

Picador

Farrar, Straus and Giroux

New York

HOW FICTION WORKS. Copyright © 2008, 2018 by James Wood.
All rights reserved. Printed in the United States
of America. For information, address Picador,
175 Fifth Avenue, New York, N.Y. 10010.

picadorusa.com • instagram.com/picador
twitter.com/picadorusa • facebook.com/picadorusa

Picador® is a U.S. registered trademark and is used by Macmillan
Publishing Group, LLC, under license from Pan Books Limited.

For book club information, please visit facebook.com/picadorbookclub
or email marketing@picadorusa.com

Designed by Jonathan D. Lippincott

The Library of Congress has cataloged
the previous Picador edition as follows:

Wood, James, 1965–
    How fiction works / James Wood. — 1st Picador ed.
    p. cm.
    Includes bibliographical references and index.
    ISBN: 978-0-312-42847-1 (trade paperback)
    ISBN: 978-1-4299-0865-8 (ebook)
    1. Fiction—Authorship.   2. Fiction—Technique.
    3. Fiction—History and Criticism.   I. Title.
PN3355.W66   2009
808.3—dc22

                                            2009001786

Picador Paperback ISBN 978-1-250-18392-7

Our book may be purchased in bulk for promotional,
educational, or business use. Please contact your local
bookseller or the Macmillan Corporate and Premium Sales
Department at 1-800-221-7945, extension 5442, or by email at
MacmillanSpecialMarkets@macmillan.com

First published in the United States by Farrar, Straus and Giroux

First Picador Edition: August 2009
Second Picador Edition: August 2018

For Norman and Elsa Rush
And for C.D.M.

*There is only one recipe—to care
a great deal for the cookery.
—Henry James*

Contents

Preface to the Tenth Anniversary Edition

In 1857, John Ruskin wrote a small book called *The Elements of Drawing*. It's a primer, an introduction, a short history; but it's also a very individual essay, full of passionate bias. It speaks to both the ordinary art lover and the better-versed painter. Above all, it is a book about looking. Ruskin begins by urging his reader to study nature—to study a leaf, say, and then to copy it in pencil. He includes his own drawing of a leaf. He moves from a leaf to a painting by Tintoretto: notice the brushstrokes, he says, see how he draws the hands, look at how he pays attention to the shading. Ruskin's authority comes not from his own authority as a draftsman, but from what his eye has seen and how well, and his ability to transmit that vision into prose.

There are surprisingly few books like this about the art of fiction—that might speak simultaneously to the common reader, the hungry writer, the student, and even the scholar. E. M. Forster's book of lectures, *Aspects of the Novel*, is deservedly famous, but it was written in 1927. I admire the critical work of Milan Kundera, of Roland Barthes, of Viktor Shklovsky, but in different ways those writers also frustrate. Kundera is a novelist and essayist rather than a practical critic; occasionally we want his hands to be a bit inkier with text. Shklovsky and Barthes, two great twentieth-century critics of narrative prose, attend brilliantly to questions of style, to words, form, codes, metaphor, and imagery. But they thought like writers who had become somewhat alienated from creative instinct, yet who were drawn, like larcenous bankers, to raid again and again the very source that sustained them— literary style. This was especially true in the case of Roland Barthes, who had a guilty love-hate relationship with novelistic realism: he was its greatest, most acutely hostile anatomist, but he couldn't stop returning to his source, to remind himself once more of all the ways it seemed fraudulent.

Shklovsky and Barthes were formalist critics: they privileged formal literary questions over political, historical, or ethical ones. Like the formalist Nabokov, they sometimes have a way of speaking about literature as if its content—what a novel is *about*—were of little consequence. Barthes concluded indeed that fictional narrative, from the referential point of view, *is* actually about nothing: "'what happens' is language alone, the adventure of language, the unceasing celebration of its coming," he wrote in 1966.

Since the 1950s, certain postmodernists, similarly hostile to the empiricist or positivist claims of realism—and taking as their example Flaubert's dream of writing a novel "about nothing," a book with no matter in it, held together only by style—have put Barthes's theoretical admonitions into practice.

But Virginia Woolf wisely reminded her readers that novelists write not only in sentences but also in paragraphs and chapters, by which she meant, I think, that novels can't be only fine assemblages of words, can't succeed if they are *only* strings of "beautiful sentences." She understood that fiction also has an ethical form, and that the form of this ethics is constituted both by a writer's style and by a novel's substance; this is how the novel justifies itself as a species of moral enquiry, what Ford Madox Ford called "a medium of profoundly serious investigation into the human case."

As I understand literature, everything is at once a moral question and a formal one (as it surely was for Ruskin, and for Ruskin's devoted reader, Proust). The formalist is ideally very interested in matters of content, since the selection of content is always a formal dilemma. And the moralist is ideally very interested in formal devices, because these are truth-bearing devices, not just beautiful ones. Fiction is not only a

music, though there has long been aesthetic tension over the slightly tormenting question of
just how musical it should be. How stylish *should*
the novel be? Is it a mirror or a music, a camera
or a painting? Iris Murdoch reframed this old
debate by dividing contemporary fiction into the
journalistic and the crystalline—the former being the hearty, content-filled, relaxed, reporto-
rial formlessness of traditional realism, the latter
being the more self-conscious stylishness and
artifice of modern formalism.

I'm not untormented by these questions myself. But my instinct is to resolve them by re-
course to both/and, rather than either/or. In this
book, I like to move between poles rather than
plant flags. A particular novel, or particular
writer, will seem artificial and lifeless—at which
moment my critique might sound as if it's coming from the hearty journalistic camp; another
novel or writer will seem not stylish enough, not
artificial *enough*—at which moment my critique
might sound as if it's coming from the crystalline aesthete camp. (Likewise, I find that when
I'm talking to religionists, I sound like an athe-
ist, and when I'm talking to atheists, I sound
religious . . .) But at all times the writer must
be wary of the conventional, whereby novelistic
devices get flattened into an easy, lazy grammar, and writing resembles some hideous old

boarding school that has never seen a compelling reason to change any of its rules.

When this book was first published in 2008, it was sometimes seen as a defense of classic realism. I hope this revised version makes clearer, ten years later, that on the contrary, I'm wary of conventional realism but drawn to a kind of deep realism, which I do believe runs through the novelistic tradition. Far from wanting to defend realism—and anyway, it needs no defense—I want to interrogate it, and to demonstrate the ways in which it is at once natural and highly artificial; I want to show how it works (and to be respectful of those mysteries that can't be explained). Of course fiction is both artifice and verisimilitude, and it isn't difficult to hold together these possibilities. *How Fiction Works* was not, in fact, the title I had originally chosen; it was *The Nearest Thing to Life*, from an essay by George Eliot on German realism, in which she says that "Art is the nearest thing to life; it is a mode of amplifying experience and extending our contact with our fellow-men beyond the bounds of our personal lot." I like this phrase, because the great Victorian realist is being precise. Art isn't the same as life, but very close to it, and that apparently slight distance ("nearest thing") is actually a canyon, the large distance of artifice.

So this book is an exercise in formalist criticism *and* an exercise in ethical criticism. I'm excited by questions of style (how metaphors work, which details are more powerful than others and why, how point of view functions, and so on) and equally excited by questions of content (what is this novel about, what does it tell us about human motive, about how we live) or literary metaphysics (what makes a novelistic character seem alive, how *does* the novel disclose the real, what is the nature of the fictional enquiry into consciousness, what *is* "the real" anyway, and so on). Most of these are old literary questions, but my hope is to answer them practically, as Ruskin approached the leaf and the Tintoretto painting—or to put it differently, I want to answer a critic's questions with a writer's answers.

And there are many answers. Readers rightly dislike the idea of being told, from on high, "how fiction works," as if there were one kind of fiction and one kind of explanation. There isn't, because the history of the novel is a history of exceptions, of books that gloriously won't *fit*. How could it be otherwise, for a tradition in which Tolstoy could claim that *War and Peace* was "not a novel"? As there are many varieties of fiction, so there are many ways (more or less fumbling and partial) of trying to describe and anatomize that variety. I might as well have called my book *How Some Fiction I Like a Lot Tends to Work*. (Though I was doubtless tempted to call it *He Knew He Was Right*.) To that end, I deliberately immerse myself and the reader in storms of quotation—page after page of examples. The idea isn't to intimidate, but to show and show and show; to honor the idea of criticism as, above all, the art of passionate re-description; to say to the reader, again and again, "Here! Look! It's like this! Or this. Or this." I take seriously Walter Benjamin's ideal: a critical book made up only of quotation, a generous anthology of re-presentation.

How Fiction Works is not a textbook, nor a history; it is very personal, and reflects its author's biases and limitations. I wanted to write an essay that resembled the kind of criticism I loved reading when I first discovered it, before university—partial, even polemical in places; argumentative, passionate, sometimes ecstatic; emanating not from the study but blowing in from life; the kind of thing written by Hazlitt and Coleridge and Woolf and Ford Madox Ford and Orwell. A textbook about the novel would have had a chapter about "plot." But because I felt I had nothing very interesting to say about plot (along with a prejudice against heavy or manipulative plotting in fiction), I chose to pass over it. Yet *How Fiction Works* has now been assigned, as a kind of textbook, in many creative writing and literature courses, so it seemed worthwhile to take the chance to revise and update it here and there. I have added a new chapter on form—on the possibilities and uses of form (a way, I guess, of writing about plot without actually writing about plot), and I have added new paragraphs and commentary on a number of contemporary writers, including, among others, Jenny Offill, Teju Cole, Ali Smith, Karl Ove Knausgaard, Elena Ferrante, Lydia Davis, and Alejandro Zambra.

These writers have all been productive since 2007, when I was writing the first edition, and their newer work excites and intrigues me. Fiction has been invigorated in the last decade by a new energy around questions of realism. Again and again, serious contemporary writers express their wariness of, dissatisfaction with, hostility to, or weariness with novelistic convention. They want to break the forms, do something different. The impulse isn't particularly new, though it's hardly invalidated by the lack of novelty. For a century or longer, the novel has been blamed, in repeated spasms of correction, for ossified convention: for the paraphernalia of plot, the rigid doxology of "conflict," development, epiphany, scene-setting, dialogue, and so on, and for the fraudulent transparency of realism. I call this liturgy of conventional ways of writing, "novelism."

These corrective energies have resulted in interesting, brilliant work—certainly from the writers I mentioned above, and also from people like Sheila Heti, Nicole Krauss, Aleksandar Hemon, Geoff Dyer, Ben Lerner, Zadie Smith, Javier Marías, Jenny Erpenbeck, among many others. Perhaps these writers have less confidence in the exact shape of their revolutionary solutions than their modernist and postmodern predecessors did. They probably don't feel like revolutionaries. But they know what they don't want to do. (The Sex Pistols' great lines rise up: "Don't know what I want/But I know how to get it.") And these days, their fiercest disaffection is reserved for the artificiality or secondhandedness of make-believe, with its reliance on manufactured otherness (that is, its reliance on invented characters who are very different from the author). The British novelist David Szalay sounds the contemporary complaint when he tells an interviewer that "I sat down to think about writing a new book and just didn't see the point of it. What's a novel? You make up a story and then you tell that story. I didn't understand why or how that would be meaningful." The Canadian writer Sheila Heti says something similar: "I'm less interested in writing about fictional people, because it seems so tiresome to make up a fake person and put them through the paces of a fake story. I just—I can't do it." Heti's solution was to write what she called "a novel from life"; her book, *How Should a Person Be?* (2010), uses transcribed conversations and actual emails. Parts of it are written out in the style of a play, other sections are essayistic. The characters appear to have been taken directly from the author's own circle of friends, and share the names of the author and her friends. Szalay's novel, *All That Man Is* (2016), divests the form of conventional plotting and presents instead a group of stories, barely bound together and striking in their journalistic immediacy. The entire book is written in an urgent, poking, present tense.

Fiction-making seems labored and obstructive because our age has a powerful "reality hunger," to borrow the title of a manifesto by David Shields*, published in the same year as Heti's novel. Shields argues against conventional fictional artifice in favor of what he calls "reality-based" art. "I find nearly all the moves the traditional novel makes unbelievably predictable, tired, contrived, and essentially purposeless," he

---

* David Shields, *Reality Hunger: A Manifesto* (2010)

writes. He has no time for characters' names, plot developments, blocks of dialogue, and the like. He prefers essays, memoirs, fragments, short stories. If he has to read novels, he likes the kind in which the author is felt as an auto-biographical presence: thinking, arguing, opin-ing. Shields is surely not alone. The literary essay, which has indeed absorbed some of the prestige of the novel form along with some of its fictive conventions, is very vital at present; there are many writers currently doing really interesting work in a generic borderland between fiction and nonfiction.

But why not try to hold together reality hunger and fiction hunger? After all, it's one thing to throw out the traditional novel, but another to throw out fictionality *tout court*, as Shields does. I, too, like reading books of fragments, aphorisms, philosophy, essays by writers that move between fiction, autobiography, and critique—Nietzsche, Pessoa, Barthes, Cioran, Primo Levi's *The Periodic Table*, Knausgaard, Maggie Nelson's *The Argonauts*, and so on. There's a special charge in such writers, some-thing immediate and personal and con-temporary. Knausgaard calls these "books that just consisted of a voice, the voice of your own personality, a life, a face, a gaze you could meet." But isn't it also beautiful, at times, to encounter material that has been invented, to meet not a familiar gaze but the visage of something that has been made out of nothing? I often think, as I open a new novel, *before this novel existed, there was nothing.* Someone created it. Out of thinnest air. This creation out of nothing has, I feel, a sacred aspect. And fictional form can also have about it a useful quality of "religious" (that's to say, moral) exercise. We rightly tire of seeing invented characters, in predictable novels, put through what Sheila Heti calls "the paces of a fake story." But the pressure of that formal testing ideally exerts a moral pressure, too. Invented dilemmas—that's essentially what fiction is—can feel strangely meaningful precisely because someone is being put through paces which are not our own, and which *have no reason to be.* Having no reason to be, these invented dilemmas must justify, aesthetically, their own invention, which then puts those fictional paces through a further set of ethical paces. When we readers ask, as we invariably do, the important aesthetic-ethical questions—"What's morally at stake here? Does this novel earn its existence? Do I believe in it aesthetically, do I grant its right to exist?"—we are putting fiction through its own paces. In this sense, fiction is a hypothesis that is always testing itself.

Moreover, in certain artworks, the otherness

of fictionalized form is a precious thing. The three-minute songs we hear on the radio and listen to on our phones are part of the tempo of our daily lives and bleed in and out of those lives (the fade-out being the perfect formal emblem of this bleed); they are continuous with our minutes and hours, and have been since we were teenagers. We will never forsake them. But there are works of art that also insist on a shimmering or almost spectral autonomy; we are overwhelmed by their sheer majestic difference, their separateness: a poem by Louise Glück, a Beethoven piano sonata or Bartók's third piano concerto, a Bresson film, novels by Ondaatje, Sebald, Kawabata, Marguerite Dumas. You know the kind of rare autonomy I am describing: it is bound up with invention, if not exactly with fictionality. Such pieces will not be so easily linked to our own lives. The author is not readily visible or audible; there is no familiar gaze. They have nothing to say about Donald Trump, thank God! They are discontinuous with our own times. Perhaps they seem almost to turn away from us.

And on the other side, what could it mean to promote "reality" over fictional artifice? I like precisely the *reality* of fictionality. The fiction I return to, year after year, already has an enormous power of reality: a hunger and an ability to satisfy hunger. (I'm thinking of Dostoevsky, Hamsun, Chekhov, Woolf, Pavese, Christina Stead, V. S. Naipaul, Spark, Bellow, Lydia Davis, Thomas Bernhard. Provide your own names.) Whose work has greater "reality-power" than Shakespeare's? What about the reality of *The Magic Mountain*? Or *The Castle*? I can't think of a novel with a more beautiful reality hunger than *A House for Mr. Biswas*. (Oh, in fact I can: Christina Stead's ravenous and ravaging novel *The Man Who Loved Children*.) And couldn't Tolstoy, perhaps the greatest novelist, also be called the greatest "reality-artist"? Tolstoy was probably not joking when he said that he lacked imagination—he did indeed copy down a great deal from life. When you first read Tolstoy, you feel as if tight clothes are being undone. The nineteenth-century novelistic conventions have fallen away: coincidence, eavesdropping, kindly benefactors, foundling babies, cruel wills, and so on. All gone. That's a large part of his "reality effect." There may be no greater piece of reality art than *The Death of Ivan Ilyich*—an excruciating, seventy-page account, still unmatched in fictional *or nonfictional* literature, of a man's illness and slow death.

"Reality hunger" is an unwittingly apt phrase, because in fact the history of the novel suggests that novelistic realism is perpetually hungry, and has kept on attempting new ways—every fifty years or so—to break into the larder, in order to pilfer some more reality-food. The writer who is seeking "life," who is trying to write "from life," is always unappeased, because no form can ever be real enough. This hunger is shared by most writers, not only by those hostile to conventional fiction-making. In the last few years, two writers (their early work championed by me, as it happens) have dominated discussion around fiction and its possibilities and pleasures: Elena Ferrante and Karl Ove Knausgaard. They are often mentioned together, though they are surely very different. Knausgaard's *My Struggle* is a six-volume autobiographical novel, more autobiography than novel, a project that seeks to explode many of the assumptions of traditional fiction-making. In it, the author is a constant autobiographical presence; the narrated facts, though of course a mixture of the recalled and invented, closely follow the author's life; in place of traditional plotting, Knausgaard instead reaches into the smallest units of the real. Like some dementedly brave anti-Flaubertian, he is unafraid of banality, naivety, cliché, sentimentality, and bad prose. Ferrante, on the other hand, writes pseudonymously, and relatively conventionally. Her Neapolitan quartet treats the stories of invented characters, and though it makes space for authorial reflection and opinion (for instance on feminist theory), it is traditionally plotted and structured. In the first novel of this quartet, *My Brilliant Friend*, a considerable power of novelistic artifice went into creating a fictionalized Naples of the 1950s—a reality effect so powerful that early readers (myself included) assumed, probably mistakenly, that the pseudonymous author must be writing autobiographically.

One of these writers is endlessly interviewed and profiled and photographed, and reads from his work all over the world; the other is not who she claims to be, and is completely invisible (despite misguided journalistic attempts to out her). One is *essentially* an autobiographer, the other *essentially* a novelist. One writes about a real man, the other about invented women. Yet both are often discussed as if they belong together. Why? The nearest explanation may be that in both their work, the reader feels a refreshingly radical innocence, a determination to use writing to uncover truth, an interest in renovating or even breaking the traditional forms while not giving up on the traditional project of realism, ever-greedy for life. These two writers see no need to choose between a reality hunger or a fiction hunger (Knausgaard is full of artifice, Ferrante full of reality). Their project, their goal, their quarry, is what Ferrante calls "authenticity," which she contrasts with mere verisimilitude.[*]

And the methods differ but the result is the same: "a medium of profoundly serious investigation into the human case."

August 2018

---

[*]Elena Ferrante, *Frantumaglia: A Writer's Journey* (2016): "The true heart of every story is its literary truth, and that is there or not there, and if it's not there, no technical skill can give it to you. You ask me about male writers who describe women with authenticity. I don't know whom to point you to. There are some who do it with verisimilitude, which is very different, however, from authenticity."

How Fiction Works

Narrating

1

The house of fiction has many windows, but only two or three doors. I can tell a story in the third person or in the first person, and perhaps in the second person singular, or in the first person plural, though successful examples of these latter two are rare,* indeed. And that is it. Anything else probably will not much resemble narration; it may be closer to poetry, or prose-poetry.

2

In reality, we are stuck with third- and first-person narration. The common idea is that there is a contrast between reliable narration (third-person omniscience) and unreliable narration (the unreliable first-person narrator, who knows less about himself than the reader eventually does). On one side, Tolstoy, say; and on the other, Humbert Humbert or Italo Svevo's narrator, Zeno Cosini, or Bertie Wooster. Authorial

---

*See Samantha Harvey's *Dear Thief* and Eimear McBride's *A Girl Is a Half-formed Thing* for examples of this rare success.

omniscience, people assume, has had its day, much as that "vast, moth-eaten musical brocade" called religion has also had its. W. G. Sebald once said to me, "I think that fiction writing which does not acknowledge the uncertainty of the narrator himself is a form of imposture which I find very, very difficult to take. Any form of authorial writing where the narrator sets himself up as stagehand and director and judge and executor in a text, I find somehow unacceptable. I cannot bear to read books of this kind." Sebald continued: "If you refer to Jane Austen, you refer to a world where there were set standards of propriety which were accepted by everyone. Given that you have a world where the rules are clear and where one knows where trespassing begins, then I think it is legitimate, within that context, to be a narrator who knows what the rules are and who knows the answers to certain questions. But I think these certainties have been taken from us by the course of history, and that we do have to acknowledge our own sense of ignorance and of insufficiency in these matters and therefore to try and write accordingly."*

*This interview can be found in *The New Brick Reader*, ed. Tara Quinn (2013).

3

For Sebald, and for many writers like him, standard third-person omniscient narration is a kind of antique cheat. But both sides of this division have been caricatured.

4

Actually, first-person narration is generally more reliable than unreliable; and third-person "omniscient" narration is generally more partial than omniscient.

The first-person narrator is often highly reliable; Jane Eyre, a highly reliable first-person narrator, for instance, tells us her story from a position of belated enlightenment (years later, married to Mr. Rochester, she can now see her whole life story, rather as Mr. Rochester's eyesight is gradually returning at the end of the novel). Even the apparently unreliable narrator is more often than not reliably unreliable. Think of Kazuo Ishiguro's butler in *The Remains of the Day*, or of Bertie Wooster, or even of Humbert Humbert. We know that the narrator is being unreliable because the author is alerting us, through reliable manipulation, to that narrator's unreliability. A process of authorial flagging is going on; the novel teaches us how to read its narrator.

Unreliably unreliable narration is very rare, actually—about as rare as a genuinely mysterious, truly bottomless character. The nameless narrator of Knut Hamsun's *Hunger* is highly unreliable, and finally unknowable (it helps that he is insane); Dostoevsky's narrator in *Notes from Underground* is the model for Hamsun. Italo Svevo's Zeno Cosini may be the best example of truly unreliable narration. He imagines that by telling us his life story he is psychoanalyzing himself (he has promised his analyst to do this). But his self-comprehension, waved confidently before our eyes, is as comically perforated as a bullet-holed flag.

5

On the other side, omniscient narration is rarely as omniscient as it seems. To begin with, authorial style generally has a way of making third-person omniscience seem partial and inflected. Authorial style tends to draw our attention toward the writer, toward the artifice of the author's construction, and so toward the writer's own impress. Thus the almost comic paradox of Flaubert's celebrated wish that the author be "impersonal," Godlike, and removed, in contrast with the high personality of his very style, those exquisite sentences and details, which are nothing less than God's showy signatures on every page: so much for the impersonal author. Tolstoy comes closest to a canonical idea of authorial omniscience, and he uses with great naturalness and authority a mode of writing that Roland Barthes called "the reference code" (or sometimes "the cultural code"), whereby a writer makes confident appeal to a universal or consensual truth, or a body of shared cultural or scientific knowledge.*

6

So-called omniscience is almost impossible. As soon as someone tells a story about a character, narrative seems to want to bend itself around that character, wants to merge with that character, to take on his or her way of thinking and speaking. A novelist's omniscience soon enough becomes a kind of secret sharing; this is called

---

*Barthes uses this term in his book *S/Z* (1970; translated by Richard Miller, 1974). He means the way that nineteenth-century writers refer to commonly accepted cultural or scientific knowledge, for instance shared ideological generalities about "women." I extend the term to cover any kind of authorial generalization. For instance, an example from Tolstoy: at the start of *The Death of Ivan Ilyich*, three of Ivan Ilyich's friends are reading his obituary, and Tolstoy writes that each man, "as is usual in such cases, was secretly congratulating himself that it was Ivan who had died and not him." *As is usual in such cases*: the author refers with ease and wisdom to a central human truth, serenely gazing into the hearts of three different men.

"free indirect style," a term novelists have lots of different nicknames for—"close third person," or "going into character."*

7

   a. He looked over at his wife. "She looks so unhappy," he thought, "almost sick." He wondered
   what to say.

This is direct or quoted speech ("'She looks so unhappy,' he thought") combined with the character's reported or indirect speech ("He wondered what to say"). The old-fashioned notion of a character's thought as a speech made to himself, a kind of internal address.

   b. He looked over at his wife. She looked so unhappy, he thought, almost sick. He wondered what
   to say.

This is reported or indirect speech, the internal speech of the husband reported by the author, and flagged as such ("he thought"). It is the most recognizable, the most habitual, of all the codes of standard realist narrative.

---

*I like D. A. Miller's phrase for free indirect style, from his book *Jane Austen, or The Secret of Style* (2003): "close writing."

c. He looked at his wife. Yes, she was tiresomely unhappy again, almost sick. What the hell should he say?

This is free indirect speech or style: the husband's internal speech or thought has been freed of its authorial flagging; no "he said to himself" or "he wondered" or "he thought."

Note the gain in flexibility. The narrative seems to float away from the novelist and take on the properties of the character, who now seems to "own" the words. The writer is free to inflect the reported thought, to bend it around the character's own words ("What the hell should he say?"). We are close to stream of consciousness, and that is the direction free indirect style takes in the nineteenth and early-twentieth centuries: "He looked at her. Unhappy, yes. Sickly. Obviously a big mistake to have told her. His stupid conscience again. Why did he blurt it? All his own fault, and what now?"

You will note that such internal monologue, freed from flagging and quotation marks, sounds very much like the pure soliloquy of eighteenth- and nineteenth-century novels (an example of a technical improvement merely renovating, in a circular manner, an original technique too basic and useful—too real—to do without).

8

Free indirect style is at its most powerful when hardly visible or audible: "Jen watched the orchestra through stupid tears." In my example, the word "stupid" marks the sentence as written in free indirect style. Remove it, and we have standard reported thought: "Jen watched the orchestra through tears." The addition of the word "stupid" raises the question: Whose word is this? It's unlikely that I would want to call my character stupid merely for listening to some music in a concert hall. No, in a marvelous alchemical transfer, the word now belongs partly to Jen. She is listening to the music and crying, and is embarrassed—we can imagine her furiously rubbing her eyes—that she has allowed these "stupid" tears to fall. Convert it back into first-person speech, and we have this: "'Stupid to be crying at this silly piece of Brahms, she thought." But this example is several words longer; and we have lost the complicated presence of the author.

9

What is so useful about free indirect style is that in our example a word like "stupid" somehow belongs both to the author and the character; we are not entirely sure who "owns" the word. Might "stupid" reflect a slight asperity or distance on the part of the author? Or does the word belong *wholly* to the character, with the author, in a rush of sympathy, having "handed" it, as it were, to the tearful woman?

10

Thanks to free indirect style, we see things through the character's eyes and language but also through the author's eyes and language. We inhabit omniscience and partiality at once. A gap opens between author and character, and the bridge—which is free indirect style itself—between them simultaneously closes that gap and draws attention to its distance.

This is merely another definition of dramatic irony: to see through a character's eyes while being encouraged to see more than the character can see (an unreliability identical to the unreliable first-person narrator's).

11

Some of the purest examples of irony are found in children's literature, which often needs to allow a child—or the child's proxy, an animal—to see the world through limited eyes, while alerting the older reader to this limitation. In

Robert McCloskey's *Make Way for Ducklings*,
Mr. and Mrs. Mallard are trying out the Boston
Public Garden for their new home, when a swan
boat (a boat made to look like a swan but actually powered by a pedal-pushing human pilot)
passes them. Mr. Mallard has never seen anything like this before. McCloskey falls naturally into free indirect style: "Just as they were
getting ready to start on their way, a strange
enormous bird came by. It was pushing a boat
full of people, and there was a man sitting on
its back. 'Good morning,' quacked Mr. Mallard,
being polite. The big bird was too proud to answer." Instead of telling us that Mr. Mallard
could make no sense of the swan boat, McCloskey places us in Mr. Mallard's confusion; yet the
confusion is obvious enough that a broad ironic
gap opens between Mr. Mallard and the reader
(or author). *We* are not confused in the same way
as Mr. Mallard; but we are also being made to
inhabit Mr. Mallard's confusion.

12

What happens, though, when a more serious
writer wants to open a very small gap between
character and author? What happens when a
novelist wants us to inhabit a character's confusion, but will not "correct" that confusion, re-

fuses to make clear what a state of nonconfusion would look like? We can walk in a straight line from McCloskey to Henry James. There is a technical connection, for instance, between *Make Way for Ducklings* and James's novel *What Maisie Knew*. Free indirect style helps us to inhabit juvenile confusion, this time a young girl's rather than a duck's. James tells the story, from the third person, of Maisie Farange, a little girl whose parents have viciously divorced. She is bounced between them, as new governesses, from each parental side, are thrust upon her. James wants us to live inside her confusion, and also wants to describe adult corruption from the eyes of childish innocence. Maisie likes one of her governesses, the plain and distinctly lower-middle-class Mrs. Wix, who wears her hair rather grotesquely, and who once had a little daughter called Clara Matilda, a girl who, at around Maisie's age, was knocked down on the Harrow Road, and is buried in the cemetery at Kensal Green. Maisie knows that her elegant and vapid mother does not think much of Mrs. Wix, but Maisie likes her all the same:

It was on account of these things that mamma got her for such low pay, really for nothing: so much, one day when Mrs. Wix had accompanied her into the drawing-room and left her, the child heard one of the ladies she found there—a lady with eyebrows arched like skipping-ropes and thick black stitching, like ruled lines for musical notes on beautiful white gloves—announce to another. She knew governesses were poor; Miss Overmore was unmentionably and Mrs. Wix ever so publicly so. Neither this, however, nor the old brown frock nor the diadem nor the button, made a difference for Maisie in the charm put forth through everything, the charm of Mrs. Wix's conveying that somehow, in her ugliness and her poverty, she was peculiarly and soothingly safe; safer than any one in the world, than papa, than mamma, than the lady with the arched eyebrows; safer even, though so much less beautiful, than Miss Overmore, on whose loveliness, as she supposed it, the little girl was faintly conscious that one couldn't rest with quite the same tucked-in and kissed-for-good-night feeling. Mrs. Wix was as safe as Clara Matilda, who was in heaven and yet, embarrassingly, also in Kensal Green, where they had been together to see her little huddled grave.

This is tremendously subtle. It is so flexible, so capable of inhabiting different levels of comprehension and irony, so full of poignant identification with young Maisie, yet constantly moving in toward Maisie and moving away from her, back toward the author.

13

James's free indirect style allows us to inhabit at least three different perspectives at once: the official parental and adult judgment on Mrs. Wix; Maisie's version of the official view; and Maisie's view of Mrs. Wix. The official view, overheard by Maisie, is filtered through Maisie's own half-comprehending voice: "It was on account of these things that mamma got her for such low pay, really for nothing." The lady with the arched eyebrows who uttered this cruelty is being paraphrased by Maisie, and paraphrased not especially skeptically or rebelliously, but with a child's wide-eyed respect for authority. James must make us feel that Maisie knows a lot but not enough. Maisie may not like the woman with the arched eyebrows who spoke thus about Mrs. Wix, but she is still in fear of her judgment, and we can hear a kind of excited respect in the narration; the free indirect style is done so well that it is *pure voice*—it longs to be turned back into the speech of which it is the paraphrase: we can hear, as a sort of shadow, Maisie saying to the kind of friend she in fact painfully lacks, "You know, mamma got her for very low pay because she is very poor and has a dead daughter. I've visited the grave, don't you know!"

So there is the official adult opinion of Mrs. Wix; and there is Maisie's comprehension of this official disapproval; and then, counter-vailingly, there is Maisie's own, much warmer opinion of Mrs. Wix, who may not be as elegant as her predecessor, Miss Overmore, but who seems much more safe: the purveyor of a uniquely "tucked-in and kissed-for-good-night feeling." (Notice that in the interest of letting Maisie "speak" through his language, James is willing to sacrifice his own stylistic elegance in a phrase like this.)

14

James's genius gathers in one word: "embarrass-ingly." That is where all the stress comes to rest. "Mrs. Wix was as safe as Clara Matilda, who was in heaven and yet, *embarrassingly*, also in Kensal Green, where they had been together to see her little huddled grave." Whose word is "embar-rassingly"? It is Maisie's: it is embarrassing for a child to witness adult grief, and embarrassing that a body could be both up in heaven and solidly in the ground. We can imagine Maisie standing next to Mrs. Wix in the cemetery at Kensal Green—it is characteristic of James's narration that he has not mentioned the place name Kensal Green until now, leaving it for us to work out—we can imagine her standing next to Mrs. Wix and feeling awkward and embar-

rassed, at once impressed by and a little afraid
of Mrs. Wix's grief. And here is the greatness of
the passage: Maisie, despite her greater love for
Mrs. Wix, stands in the same relation to
Mrs. Wix as she stands to the lady with the
arched eyebrows; both women cause her some
embarrassment. She fully understands neither,
even if she uncomprehendingly prefers the former. "Embarrassingly": the word encodes Maisie's
natural embarrassment and also the internalized
embarrassment of official adult opinion ("My
dear, it is so *embarrassing*, that woman is always
taking her up to Kensal Green!").

15

Remove the word "embarrassingly" from the
sentence and it would barely be free indirect
style: "Mrs. Wix was as safe as Clara Matilda,
who was in heaven and yet also in Kensal Green,
where they had been together to see her little
huddled grave." The addition of the single adverb takes us deep into Maisie's confusion, and
at that moment we become her—that adverb is
passed from James to Maisie, is given to Maisie.
We merge with her. Yet, within the same sentence, having briefly merged, we are drawn back:
"her little *huddled* grave." "Embarrassingly" is
the word Maisie might have used, but "huddled"

is not. It is Henry James's word. The sentence pulsates, moves in and out, toward the character and away from her—when we reach "huddled" we are reminded that an *author* allowed us to merge with his character, that the author's magniloquent style is the envelope within which this generous contract is carried.

16

The critic Hugh Kenner writes about a moment in *A Portrait of the Artist as a Young Man* when Uncle Charles "repaired" to the outhouse. "Repair" is a pompous verb that belongs to outmoded poetic convention. It is "bad" writing. Joyce, with his acute eye for cliché, would only use such a word knowingly. It must be, says Kenner, Uncle Charles's word, the word he might use about himself in his fond fantasy about his own importance ("And so I *repair* to the outhouse"). Kenner names this the Uncle Charles principle. Mystifyingly, he calls this "something new in fiction." Yet we know it isn't. The Uncle Charles principle is just an edition of free indirect style. Joyce is a master at it. "The Dead" begins like this: "Lily, the caretaker's daughter, was literally run off her feet." But no one is *literally* run off her feet. What we hear is Lily saying to herself or to a friend (with great emphasis on precisely the most inaccurate word, and with a strong accent): "Oi was *lit-er-rully* ron off me feet!"

17

Even if Kenner's example is a bit different, it is still not new. Mock-heroic poetry of the eighteenth century gets its laughs by applying the language of epic or the Bible to reduced human subjects. In Pope's *The Rape of the Lock*, Belinda's makeup and dressing-table effects are seen as "unnumbered treasures," "India's glowing gems," "all Arabia breathes from yonder box," and so on. Part of the joke is that this is the kind of language that the personage—"personage" being precisely a mock-heroic word—might want to use about herself; the rest of the joke resides in the actual littleness of that personage. Well, what is this but an early form of free indirect style?

In the opening of Chapter 5 of *Pride and Prejudice*, Jane Austen introduces us to Sir William Lucas, once the mayor of Longbourn, who, knighted by the king, has decided that he is too big for the town, and must move to a new pile:

Sir William Lucas had been formerly in trade in Meryton, where he had made a tolerable fortune,

and risen to the honour of knighthood by an address
to the King, during his mayoralty. The distinction
had perhaps been felt too strongly. It had given him
a disgust to his business and to his residence in a
small market town; and quitting them both, he had
removed with his family to a house about a mile
from Meryton, denominated from that period Lucas Lodge, where he could think with pleasure of his
own importance . . .

Austen's irony dances over this like the long-
legged fly in Yeats's poem: "where he had made
a tolerable fortune." What is, or would be, a "tolerable" fortune? Intolerable to whom, tolerated
by whom? But the great example of mock-heroic
comedy resides in that phrase "denominated
from that period Lucas Lodge." Lucas Lodge is
funny enough; it is like Toad of Toad Hall or
Shandy Hall, or Trump Tower, and we can be
sure that the house does not quite measure up
to its alliterative grandeur. But the pomposity
of "denominated from that period" is funny
because we can imagine Sir William saying to
himself "and I will *denominate* the house, from
this period, Lucas Lodge. Yes, that sounds *prodi-
gious.*" Mock-heroic is almost identical, at this
point, to free indirect style. Austen has handed
the language over to Sir William, but she is still
tartly in control.

A modern master of the mock-heroic is V. S. Naipaul in *A House for Mr Biswas*: "When he got home he mixed and drank some Maclean's Brand Stomach Powder, undressed, got into bed and began to read Epictetus." The comic-pathetic capitalization of the brand name, and the presence of Epictetus—Pope himself would not have done it better. And what is the make of the bed that poor Mr. Biswas rests on? It is, Naipaul deliberately tells us every so often, a "Slumberking bed": the right name for a man who may be a king or little god in his own mind but who will never rise above "Mr." And Naipaul's decision, of course, to refer to Biswas as "Mr. Biswas" throughout the novel has itself a mock-heroic irony about it, "Mr." being at once the most ordinary honorific and, in a poor society, a by no means spontaneous achievement. "Mr. Biswas," we might say, is free indirect style in a pod: "Mr." is how Biswas likes to think of himself; but it is all he will ever be, along with everyone else.

18

There is a funny moment in Penelope Fitzgerald's novel, *The Blue Flower*—one of many in that gemlike book. Fitzgerald has established a comic contrast between the rapturous, self-absorbed, romantic dreamer, Fritz von Hardenberg (based on the German poet and philosopher, Novalis), and his friend, Karoline Just, who is sensible, sober, and humanly wise. In the gendered environment of late-eighteenth-century Prussia, Karoline's modest task is to be a domestic helpmate, while Fritz's grander, male role is to talk and explain: philosophy, science, poetry, and love. But the canny author, channeling her inner Jane Austen, observes this setup with an ironic eye. The two are talking in the kitchen: "All was confessed, he talked perpetually. Neither the sewing nor the forewinter sausage-chopping deterred him. As she chopped, Karoline learned that the world is tending day by day not towards destruction, but towards infinity. She was told where Fichte's philosophy fell short." As the woman works, the man talks. But where, precisely, does the irony fall? Surely on that innocent-sounding verb, "learned": as she chops sausages, Karoline *learns* that the world is tending toward infinity. But she hasn't actually learned it; she's been *told* it—a rather different thing—by her exuberant, mansplaining instructor. You can't *learn*, in a few seconds in the kitchen, something as massive and amorphous as the "fact" that the world tends towards infinity. Elsewhere in the novel, women are amusedly ironic or briskly sardonic when Fritz starts opining. At one moment, he announces that a heroine in a

Goethe novel dies because the world "is not holy enough to contain her." To which Karoline tartly responds: "She dies because Goethe couldn't think what to do with her next." So we can assume, I think, that "she learned" is being used at Fritz's expense. The sentence really means: "Karoline was told, and tried to learn, but finally did not learn, that the world tends toward infinity." So the verb, used as part of free indirect style, achieves here the purest form of compacted irony: it means the opposite of what is written. Free indirect style is sometimes called a conservative or old-fashioned technique,* but it is an insidiously radical literary tool, because it allows the author to put words on the page whose ironic, shadow meanings are virtual inversions of their apparent ones.

19

There is a final refinement of free indirect style— we should now just call it authorial irony—when the gap between an author's voice and a character's voice seems to collapse altogether; when a character's voice does indeed seem rebelliously to have taken over the narration altogether. "The town was small, worse than a village, and in it

---

*See, for instance, Fredric Jameson, *The Antinomies of Realism* (2013).

lived almost none but old people, who died so rarely it was even annoying." What an amazing opening! It is the first sentence of Chekhov's story "Rothschild's Fiddle." The next sentences are: "And in the hospital and jail there was very little demand for coffins. In short, business was bad." The rest of the paragraph introduces us to an extremely mean coffin-maker, and we realize that the story has opened in the middle of free indirect style: "and in it lived almost none but old people, who died so rarely it was even annoying." We are in the midst of the coffin-maker's mind, for whom longevity is an economic nuisance. Chekhov subverts the expected neutrality of the opening of a story or novel, which might traditionally begin with a panning shot before we narrow our focus ("The little town of N. was smaller than a village, and had two rather grubby little streets," etc.). But where Joyce, in "The Dead," clearly pegs his free indirect style to Lily, Chekhov begins his use of it *before* his character has even been identified. And while Joyce abandons Lily's perspective, moving first into authorial omniscience and then to Gabriel Conroy's point of view, Chekhov's story continues to narrate events from the coffin-maker's eyes.

Or perhaps it might be more accurate to say that the story is written from a point of view closer to a village chorus than to one man. This village chorus sees life pretty much as brutally as the coffin-maker would—"There were not many patients, and he did not have to wait long, only about three hours"—but continues to see this world after the coffin-maker has died. The Sicilian writer Giovanni Verga (almost exactly contemporaneous with Chekhov) used this kind of village-chorus narration much more systematically than his Russian counterpart. His stories, though written technically in authorial third person, seem to emanate from a community of Sicilian peasants; they are thick with proverbial sayings, truisms, and homely similes.

We can call this "unidentified free indirect style."

20

As a logical development of free indirect style, it is not surprising that Dickens, Hardy, Verga, Chekhov, Faulkner, Pavese, Henry Green, and others tend to produce the kinds of similes and metaphors that, while successful and literary enough in their own right, are also the kinds of similes and metaphors that their own characters might produce. When Robert Browning describes the sound of a bird singing its song twice over, in order to "recapture / The first fine careless rapture," he is being a poet, trying to find the best poetic image; but when Chekhov, in his story "Peasants," says that a bird's cry sounded as if a cow had been locked up in a shed all night, he is being a fiction writer: he is thinking like one of his peasants.

21

Seen in this light, there is almost no area of narration not touched by the long finger of free indirect narration—which is to say, by irony. Consider the penultimate chapter of Nabokov's *Pnin*: the comic Russian professor has just given a party, and has received the news that the college where he teaches no longer wants his services. He is sadly washing his dishes, and a nutcracker slips out of his soapy hand and falls into the water, apparently about to break a beautiful submerged bowl. Nabokov writes that the nutcracker falls from Pnin's hands like a man falling from a roof; Pnin tries to grasp it, but "the leggy thing" slips into the water. "Leggy thing" is a terrific metaphorical likeness: we can instantly see the long legs of the wayward nutcracker, as if it were falling off the roof and walking away. But "thing" is even better, *precisely because it is vague*: Pnin is lunging at the implement, and what word in English better conveys a messy lunge, a swipe at verbal meaning, than "thing"? Now if the brilliant "leggy" is Nabokov's word, then the hapless "thing" is Pnin's word, and Nabokov is here using a kind of free indirect style, probably without even thinking about it. As usual, if we turn it into first-person speech, we can hear the way in which the word "thing" belongs to Pnin and wants to be spoken: "Come here, you, you . . . oh . . . you annoying *thing*!" Splash.*

---

*Nabokov is a great creator of the kind of extravagant metaphors that the Russian formalists called "estranging" or defamiliarizing (a nutcracker has legs, a half-rolled black umbrella looks like a duck in deep mourning, and so on). The formalists liked the way that Tolstoy, say, insisted on seeing adult things—like war, or the opera—from a child's viewpoint, in order to make them look strange. But whereas the Russian formalists see this metaphorical habit as emblematic of the way that fiction does not refer to reality, is a self-enclosed machine (such metaphors are the jewels of the author's freakish, solipsistic art), I prefer the way that such metaphors, as in Pnin's "leggy thing," refer deeply to reality: because they emanate from the characters themselves, and are fruits of free indirect style. Shklovksy wonders out loud, in *Theory of Prose*, if Tolstoy got his technique of estrangement from French authors like Chateaubriand, but Cervantes seems much more likely—as when Sancho first arrives in Barcelona, sees on the water the galleys with their many oars, and metaphorically mistakes the oars for feet: "Sancho couldn't imagine how those hulks moving about on top of the sea could have so many feet." This is estranging metaphor as a branch of free indirect style; it makes the world look peculiar, but it makes Sancho look very familiar.

22

It is useful to watch good writers make mistakes. Plenty of excellent ones stumble at free indirect style. Free indirect style solves much, but accentuates a problem inherent in all fictional narration: Do the words these characters use seem like the words they might use, or do they sound more like the author's?

When I wrote "Jen watched the orchestra through stupid tears," the reader was prompted to assign "stupid" to the character herself. But if I had written "Jen watched the orchestra through viscous, swollen tears," the adjectives would suddenly look annoyingly authorial, as if I were trying to find the fanciest way of describing those tears.

Take John Updike in his novel *Terrorist*. On the third page of his book, he has his protagonist, a fervid eighteen-year-old American Muslim called Ahmad, walk to school along the streets of a fictionalized New Jersey town. Since the novel has hardly begun, Updike must work to establish the quiddity of his character:

> Ahmad is eighteen. This is early April; again green sneaks, seed by seed, into the drab city's earthy crevices. He looks down from his new height and thinks that to the insects unseen in the grass he would be, if they had a consciousness like his, God.

In the year past he has grown three inches, to six feet—more unseen materialist forces, working their will upon him. He will not grow any taller, he thinks, in this life or the next. *If there is a next*, an inner devil murmurs. What evidence beyond the Prophet's blazing and divinely inspired words proves that there is a next? Where would it be hidden? Who would forever stoke Hell's boilers? What infinite source of energy would maintain opulent Eden, feeding its dark-eyed houris, swelling its heavy-hanging fruits, renewing the streams and splashing fountains in which God, as described in the ninth sura of the Qur'an, takes eternal good pleasure? What of the second law of thermodynamics?

Ahmad is walking along the street, looking about, and thinking: the classic post-Flaubertian novelistic activity. The first few lines are routine enough. Then Updike wants to make the thought theological, so he effects an uneasy transition: "He will not grow any taller, he thinks, in this life or the next. *If there is a next*, an inner devil murmurs." It seems very unlikely that a schoolboy thinking about how much he had grown in the last year would think: "I shall not grow any taller, in this life or the next." The words "or the next" are there just to feed Updike a chance to write about the Islamic idea of heaven. We are only four pages in, and any attempt to follow Ahmad's own voice has been abandoned: the phrasing, syntax, and lyricism are Updike's, not Ahmad's ("Who would forever stoke Hell's boilers?"). The penultimate line is telling: "in which God, *as described in the ninth sura of the Qur'an*, takes eternal good pleasure." How willing Henry James was, by contrast, to let us inhabit Maisie's mind, and how much he squeezed into that single adverb, "embarrassingly." But Updike is unsure about entering Ahmad's mind, and crucially, unsure about *our* entering Ahmad's mind, and so he plants his big authorial flags all over his mental site. So he has to identify exactly which sura refers to God, although Ahmad would know where this appears, and would have no need to remind himself.*

23

On the one hand, the author wants to have his or her own words, wants to be the master of a personal style; on the other hand, narrative bends toward its characters and their habits of speech.

---

*As soon as we imagine a Christian version of this narration, we can gauge Updike's awkward alienation from his character. Imagine a devout Christian schoolboy walking along, and the text going something like this: "And wouldn't His will always be done, as described in the fourth line of the Lord's Prayer?" Free indirect style exists precisely to *get around* such clumsiness.

The dilemma is most acute in first-person narration, which is generally a nice hoax: the narrator pretends to speak to us, while in fact the author is writing to us, and we go along with the deception happily enough. Even Faulkner's narrators in *As I Lay Dying* rarely sound much like children or illiterates.

But the same tension is present in third-person narration, too: Who really thinks that it is Leopold Bloom, in the midst of his stream of consciousness, who notices "the flabby gush of porter" as it is poured into a drain, or appreciates "the buzzing prongs" of a fork in a restaurant—and in such fine words? These exquisite perceptions and beautifully precise phrases are Joyce's, and the reader has to make a treaty, whereby we accept that Bloom will sometimes sound like Bloom and sometimes sound more like Joyce.

This is as old as literature: Shakespeare's characters sound like themselves and always like Shakespeare, too. It is not really Cornwall who wonderfully calls Gloucester's eye a "vile jelly" before he rips it out—though Cornwall speaks the words—but Shakespeare, who has provided the phrase.

24

A contemporary writer like David Foster Wallace wants to push this tension to the limit. He writes from within his characters' voices and simultaneously over them, obliterating them in order to explore larger, if more abstract, questions of language. In this passage from his story "The Suffering Channel," he evokes the ruined argot of Manhattan media-speak:

> The other *Style* piece the associate editor had referred to concerned The Suffering Channel, a wide grid cable venture that Atwater had gotten Laurel Manderley to do an end run and pitch directly to the editor's head intern for WHAT IN THE WORLD. Atwater was one of three full time salarymen tasked to the WITW feature, which received .75 editorial pages per week, and was the closest any of the BSG weeklies got to freakshow or tabloid, and was a bone of contention at the very highest levels of *Style*. The staff size and large font specs meant that Skip Atwater was officially contracted for one 400 word piece every three weeks, except the juniormost of the WITW salarymen had been on half time ever since Eckleschafft-Böd had forced Mrs. Anger to cut the editorial budget for everything except celebrity news, so in reality it was more like three finished pieces every eight weeks.

Here is another example of what I called "un-identified free indirect style." As in the Chekhov story, the language hovers around the view-point of the character (the journalist Atwater), but really emanates from a kind of "village chorus"—it is an amalgam of the kind of lan-guage we might expect this particular commu-nity to speak if they were telling the story.

25

In Wallace's case, the language of his unidenti-fied narration is obtrusive and sometimes hard to read. No analogous problem arose for Chekhov and Verga, because they were not faced with the saturation of language by mass media. But in America, things were different: Dreiser in *Sister Carrie* (published in 1900) and Sinclair Lewis in *Babbitt* (1923) take care to reproduce in full the advertisements and business letters and commer-cial flyers they want novelistically to report on.

The risky tautology inherent in the con-temporary writing project has begun: in order to evoke a debased language (the debased lan-guage your character might use), you must be willing to represent that mangled language in your text, and perhaps thoroughly "debase" your own language. Pynchon, DeLillo, and David

Foster Wallace are to some extent Lewis's heirs
(probably in this respect only), and Wallace
pushes to parodic extremes his full-immersion
method: he does not flinch at narrating twenty
or thirty pages in the style quoted above.* His
fiction prosecutes a courageous argument about
the decomposition of language in America,
and he is not afraid to decompose—and
discompose—his own style in the interests of
making us live through this linguistic America
with him. "This is America, you live in it, you
let it happen. Let it unfurl," as Pynchon has it
in *The Crying of Lot 49*. Whitman calls America
"the greatest poem," but if this is the case then
America may represent a mimetic danger to the
writer, the bloating of one's own poem with that
rival poem, America. Auden frames the general
problem well in his poem "The Novelist": the
poet can dash forward like a hussar, he writes,
but the novelist must slow down, learn how to
be "plain and awkward," and must "become the
whole of boredom." In other words, the novelist's job is to become, to impersonate what he
describes, even when the subject itself is debased,
vulgar, boring. Wallace is good at becoming the
whole of boredom; a necessary achievement.

---

*See the brilliant, but taxing long story, "The Depressed Person," which
sinks us into the repetitive feedback loop of the "depressed person."

26

So there is a tension basic to stories and novels: Can we reconcile the author's perceptions and language with the character's perception and language? If the author and character are absolutely merged, as in the passage from Wallace above, we can sometimes feel "the whole of boredom"—the author's corrupted language just mimics an actually existing corrupted language we all know too well, and are in fact quite desperate to escape. But if author and character get too separated, as in the Updike passage, we feel the cold breath of an alienation over the text, and begin to resent the over-"literary" efforts of the stylist. The Updike is an example of aestheticism (the author gets in the way); the Wallace is an example of antiaestheticism (the character is all): but both examples are really species of the same aestheticism, which is at bottom the strenuous display of *style*.

27

So the novelist is always working with at least three languages. There is the author's own language, style, perceptual equipment, and so on; there is the character's presumed language, style, perceptual equipment, and so on; and there is what we could call the language of the world—

the language that fiction inherits before it gets
to turn it into novelistic style, the language of
daily speech, of newspapers, of offices, of advertising, of the blogosphere and text messaging. In
this sense, the novelist is a triple writer, and the
contemporary novelist now feels especially the
pressure of this tripleness, thanks to the omnivorous presence of the third horse of this troika,
the language of the world, which has invaded
our subjectivity, our intimacy, the intimacy that
James thought should be the proper quarry of
the novel, and which he called (in a troika of his
own) "the palpable present-*intimate*."*

28

Another example of the novelist writing over his
character occurs (briefly) in Saul Bellow's *Seize the
Day*. Tommy Wilhelm, the out-of-work sales-
man down on his luck, neither much of an aesthete nor an intellectual, is anxiously watching
the board at a Manhattan commodity exchange.
Next to him, an old hand named Mr. Rappaport
is smoking a cigar. "A long perfect ash formed
on the end of the cigar, the white ghost of the
leaf with all its veins and its fainter pungency.

---

*Letter to Sarah Orne Jewett, October 5, 1901, in Henry James, *Selected
Letters*, edited by Leon Edel (1974).

It was ignored, in its beauty, by the old man. For it was beautiful. Wilhelm he ignored as well."

It is a gorgeous, musical phrase, and characteristic of both Bellow and modern fictional narrative. The fiction slows down to draw our attention to a potentially neglected surface or texture—an example of a "descriptive pause,"* familiar to us when a novel halts its action and the author says, in effect, "Now I am going to tell you about the town of N., which was nestled in the Carpathian foothills," or "Jerome's house was a large dark castle, set in fifty thousand acres of rich grazing land." But at the same time it is a detail apparently seen not by the author—or not only by the author—but by a character. And this is what Bellow wobbles on; he admits an anxiety endemic to modern narrative, and which modern narrative tends to elide. The ash is noticed, and then Bellow comments: "It was ignored, in its beauty, by the old man. For it was beautiful. Wilhelm he ignored as well." *Seize the Day* is written in a very close third-person narration, a free indirect style that sees most of the action from Tommy's viewpoint. Bellow seems here to imply that Tommy notices

---

*This is Gérard Genette's term, from *Narrative Discourse: An Essay in Method*, translated by Jane E. Lewin (1980). Elmore Leonard calls these the boring parts that readers tend to skip: "If it sounds like writing, I rewrite it."

the ash, because it was beautiful, and that
Tommy, also ignored by the old man, is also in
some way beautiful. But the fact that Bellow
tells us this is surely a concession to our implied
objection: How and why would Tommy notice
this ash, and notice it so well, in *these* fine words?
To which Bellow replies, anxiously, in effect:
"Well, you might have thought Tommy incapable of such finery, but he really did notice this
fact of beauty; and that is because he is somewhat beautiful himself."

29

The tension between the author's style and his
or her characters' styles becomes acute when
three elements coincide: when a notable stylist
is at work, like Bellow or Joyce; when that stylist also has a commitment to following the perceptions and thoughts of his or her characters (a
commitment usually organized by free indirect
style or its offspring, stream of consciousness);
and when the stylist has a special interest in the
rendering of detail.

Stylishness, free indirect style, and detail: I
have described Flaubert, whose work opens up
and tries to solve this tension, and who is really
its founder.

Flaubert and Modern Narrative

30

However you feel about Flaubert (I love him and hate him in equal measure), novelists should thank him the way poets thank spring: it all begins again with him. There really is a time before Flaubert and a time after him. Flaubert established, for good or ill, what most readers think of as modern realist narration, and his influence is almost too familiar to be visible. We hardly remark of good prose that it favors the telling and brilliant detail; that it privileges a high degree of visual noticing; that it maintains an unsentimental composure and knows how to withdraw, like a good valet, from superfluous commentary; that it judges good and bad neutrally; that it seeks out the truth, even at the cost of repelling us; and that the author's fingerprints on all this are, paradoxically, traceable but not visible. You can find some of this in Defoe or Austen or Balzac, but not all of it until Flaubert.

Take the following passage, in which Frédéric Moreau, the hero of *Sentimental Education*, wanders through the Latin Quarter, alive to the sights and sounds of Paris:

He sauntered idly up the Latin Quarter, usually bustling with life but now deserted, for the students had all gone home. The great walls of the colleges looked grimmer than ever, as if the silence had made them longer; all sorts of peaceful sounds could be heard, the fluttering of wings in bird-cages, the whirring of a lathe, a cobbler's hammer; and the old-clothes men, in the middle of the street, looking hopefully but in vain at every window. At the back of the deserted cafés, women behind the bars yawned between their untouched bottles; the newspapers lay unopened on the reading-room tables; in the laundresses' workshops the washing quivered in the warm draughts. Every now and then he stopped at a bookseller's stall; an omnibus, coming down the street and grazing the pavement, made him turn round; and when he reached the Luxembourg he retraced his steps.

This was published in 1869, but might have appeared in 1969; many novelists still sound essentially the same. Flaubert seems to scan the streets indifferently, like a camera. Just as when we watch a film we no longer notice what has been excluded, what is just outside the edges of the camera frame, so we no longer notice what Flaubert chooses *not* to notice. And we no longer notice that what he *has* selected is not of course casually scanned but quite savagely chosen, that each detail is almost frozen in its gel of chosenness. How superb and magnificently isolate these details are—the women yawning, the unopened newspapers, the washing quivering in the warm air.

31

The reason that we don't, at first, notice how carefully Flaubert is selecting his details is because Flaubert is working very hard to obscure this labor from us, and is keen to hide the question of who is doing all this noticing: Flaubert or Frédéric? Flaubert was explicit about this. He wanted the reader to be faced with what he called a smooth wall of apparently impersonal prose, the details simply amassing themselves like life. "An author in his work must be like God in the universe, present everywhere and visible nowhere," he famously wrote in one of his letters, in 1852. "Art being a second nature, the creator of that nature must operate with analogous procedures: let there be felt in every atom, every aspect, a hidden, infinite impassivity. The effect on the spectator must be a kind of amazement. How did it all come about!"

To this end, Flaubert perfected a technique that is essential to realist narration: the confusing of habitual detail with dynamic detail.

Obviously, in that Paris street, the women cannot be yawning for the same length of time as the washing is quivering or the newspapers lying on the tables. Flaubert's details belong to different time signatures, some instantaneous and some recurrent, yet they are smoothed together as if they are all happening simultaneously.

The effect is lifelike—in a beautifully artificial way. Flaubert manages to suggest that these details are somehow at once important and unimportant: important because they have been noticed by him and put down on paper, and unimportant because they are all jumbled together, seen as if out of the corner of the eye; they seem to come at us "like life." From this flows a great deal of modern storytelling, such as war reportage. The crime writer and war reporter merely increase the extremity of this contrast between important and unimportant detail, converting it into a tension between the awful and the regular: a soldier dies while nearby a little boy goes to school.

32

Different time signatures were not Flaubert's invention, of course. There have always been characters doing something while something else is going on. In Book 22 of *The Iliad*, Hector's wife is at home warming his bath though he has in fact died moments before; Auden praised Breughel, in "Musée des Beaux Arts," for noticing that, while Icarus fell, a ship was calmly moving on through the waves, unnoticing. In the Dunkirk section of Ian McEwan's *Atonement*, the protagonist, a British soldier retreating through chaos and death toward Dunkirk, sees a barge going by. "Behind him, ten miles away, Dunkirk burned. Ahead, in the prow, two boys were bending over an upturned bike, mending a puncture perhaps."

Flaubert differs a bit from those examples in the *way* he insists on driving together short-term and long-term occurrences. Breughel and McEwan are describing two very different things happening at the same time; but Flaubert is asserting a temporal impossibility: that the eye— his eye, or Frédéric's eye—can witness, in one visual gulp as it were, sensations and occurrences that must be happening at different speeds and at different times. In *Sentimental Education*, when the 1848 revolution comes to Paris and the soldiers are firing on everyone and all is mayhem: "He ran all the way to the Quai Voltaire. An old man in his shirt sleeves was weeping at an open window, his eyes raised towards the sky. The Seine was flowing peacefully by. The sky was blue; birds were singing in the Tuileries." Again, the one-off occurrence of the old man at the window is dropped into the longer-term occurrences, as if they all belonged together.

33

From here, it is a small leap to the insistence, familiar in modern war reporting, that the awful and the regular will be noticed at the same time—by the fictional hero, and/or by the writer—and that in some way *there is no important difference between the two experiences*: all detail is somewhat numbing, and strikes the traumatized voyeur in the same way. Here, again, is *Sentimental Education*:

> There was firing from every window overlooking the square; bullets whistled through the air; the fountain had been pierced, and the water, mingling with blood, spread in puddles on the ground. People slipped in the mud on clothes, shakos, and weapons; Frédéric felt something soft under his foot; it was the hand of a sergeant in a grey overcoat who was lying face down in the gutter. Fresh groups of workers kept coming up, driving the fighters towards the guard-house. The firing became more rapid. The wine-merchants' shops were open, and every now and then somebody would go in to smoke a pipe or drink

a glass of beer, before returning to the fight. A stray
dog started howling. This raised a laugh.

The moment that strikes us as decisively modern in that passage is "Frédéric felt something
soft under his foot; it was the hand of a sergeant
in a grey overcoat." First the calm, terrible an-
ticipation ("something soft"), and then the calm,
terrible validation ("it was the hand of a sergeant"),
the writing refusing to become involved in the
emotion of the material. Ian McEwan systematically uses the same technique in his Dunkirk
section, and so does Stephen Crane—who read
Sentimental Education—in *The Red Badge of
Courage*:

> He was being looked at by a dead man who was
> seated with his back against a columnlike tree. The
> corpse was dressed in a uniform that once had been
> blue, but was now faded to a melancholy shade of
> green. The eyes, staring at the youth, had changed
> to the dull hue to be seen on the side of a dead fish.
> The mouth was open. Its red had changed to an ap-
> palling yellow. Over the gray skin of the face ran
> little ants. One was trundling some sort of a bun-
> dle along the upper lip.

This is even more "cinematic" than Flaubert (and
film, of course, borrows this technique from the

novel). There is the calm horror ("the dull hue to be seen on the side of a dead fish"). There is the zoomlike action of the lens, as it gets closer and closer to the corpse. But the reader is getting closer and closer to the horror, while the prose is simultaneously moving further and further back, insisting on its anti-sentimentality. There is the modern commitment to detail itself: the protagonist seems to be noticing so much, recording everything! ("One was trundling some sort of bundle along the upper lip." Would any of us actually see as much?) And there are the different time signatures: the corpse will be dead forever, but on his face, life goes on; the ants are busily indifferent to human mortality.*

---

*The ants crawling across the face represent almost a cliché of cinematic grammar. Think of the ants on the hand in Buñuel's *Un Chien andalou,* or on the ear at the start of David Lynch's *Blue Velvet.*

Flaubert and the Rise of the Flaneur

34

Flaubert can drive together his time signatures because French verb forms allow him to use the imperfect past tense to convey both discrete occurrences ("he was sweeping the road") and recurrent occurrences ("every week he swept the road"). English is clumsier, and we have to resort to "he was doing something" or "he would do something" or "he used to do something"—"every week he would sweep the road"—to translate recurrent verbs accurately. But as soon as we do that in English, we have given the game away, and are admitting the existence of different temporalities. In *Contre Sainte-Beuve*, Proust rightly saw that this use of the imperfect tense was Flaubert's great innovation. And Flaubert founds this new style of realism on his use of the eye—the authorial eye, and the character's eye. I said that Updike's Ahmad, just walking along the street noticing things and thinking thoughts, was engaged in the classic post-Flaubertian novelistic activity. Flaubert's Frédéric is a forerunner of what would later be called the flaneur—the loafer, usually a young man, who walks the streets with no great urgency, seeing, looking, reflecting. We know this type from Baudelaire,* from the all-seeing narrator of Rilke's autobiographical novel *The Notebooks of Malte Laurids Brigge*, and from Walter Benjamin's writings about Baudelaire.

35

This figure is essentially a stand-in for the author, is the author's porous scout, helplessly inundated with impressions. He goes out into the world like Noah's dove, to bring a report back. The rise of this authorial scout is intimately connected to the rise of urbanism, to the fact that huge conglomerations of mankind throw at the writer—or the designated perceiver—large, bewilderingly various amounts of detail. Jane Austen is, essentially, a rural novelist, and London, as figured in *Emma*, is really just the village of Highgate. Her heroines never idly walk along, just thinking and looking: all their thought is intensely directed to the moral problem at hand. But when Wordsworth, at around the time the young Austen was writing, visits London in *The Prelude*, he immediately begins to sound like a flaneur—like a modern novelist:

*See Baudelaire's seminal essay, "The Painter of Modern Life" (1863).

Here files of ballads dangle from dead walls,
Advertisements of giant-size, from high
Press forward in all colour on the sight . . .
A travelling Cripple, by the trunk cut short.
And stumping with his arms . . .
The Bachelor that loves to sun himself,
The military Idler, and the Dame . . .
The Italian, with his Frame of Images
Upon his head; with basket at his waist
The Jew; the stately and slow-moving Turk
With freight of slippers piled beneath his arm.

Wordsworth goes on to write that if we tire of "random sights," we can find in the crowd "all specimens of man":

Through all the colours which the sun bestows,
And every character of form and face,
The Swede, the Russian; from the genial South,
The Frenchman and the Spaniard; from remote
America, the Hunter-Indian; Moors,
Malays, Lascars, the Tartar and Chinese,
And Negro Ladies in white muslin gowns.

Notice how Wordsworth, like Flaubert, adjusts the lens of his optic as he pleases: we have several lines of generalized cataloging (the Swede, the Russian, the American, etc.), but we end with a sudden plucking of a single color contrast: "And Negro

Ladies in white muslin gowns." The writer zooms
in and out at will, but these details, despite their
differences in focus and intensity, are pushed at
us, as if by the croupier's stick, in one single heap.

36

Wordsworth is looking himself at these aspects
of London. He is being a poet, writing about
himself. The novelist wants to record details like
this, too, but it is harder to act like a lyric poet
in the novel, because you have to write through
other people, and then we are returned to our
basic novelistic tension: Is it the novelist who is
noticing these things or the fictional character?
In that first passage from *Sentimental Education*,
is Flaubert doing a bit of nice Parisian scene-
setting, with the reader assuming that Frédéric
is seeing perhaps a *few* of the details in the paragraph while Flaubert sees all of them in his mind's
eye; or is the entire passage essentially written in
loose free indirect style, with the assumption that
Frédéric notices *everything* Flaubert draws our attention to—the unopened newspapers, the
women yawning, and so on? Flaubert tries hard to
make this question unnecessary, to so confuse author and flaneur that the reader unconsciously
raises Frédéric up to the stylistic level of Flaubert:

both must be pretty good, we decide, at noticing things, and we are content to leave it there.

Flaubert needs to do this because he is at once a realist and a stylist, a reporter and a poet manqué. The realist wants to record a great deal, to do a Balzacian number on Paris. But the stylist is not content with Balzacian jumble and verve; he wants to discipline this welter of detail, to turn it into immaculate sentences and images: Flaubert's letters speak of the effort of trying to turn prose into poetry.* We nowadays more or less assume, so strong is the post-Flaubertian inflection of our era, that a fancy stylist must sometimes write over his or her characters (as in the example from Updike and the one from Wallace); or that they may appoint a surrogate: Humbert Humbert famously announces that he has a fancy prose style, as a way, surely, of explaining his

---

*The differences between Balzacian and Flaubertian realism are three-fold: First, Balzac of course notices a great deal in his fiction, but the emphasis is always on abundance rather than intense selectivity of detail. Second, Balzac has no special commitment to free indirect style or authorial impersonality, and feels wonderfully free to break in as the author/narrator, with essays and digressions and bits of social information. (He seems decidedly eighteenth-century in this respect.) Third, and following on from these two differences: he has no distinctively Flaubertian interest in blurring the question of *who* is noticing all this stuff. For these reasons, I see Flaubert and not Balzac as the real founder of modern fictional narrative.

creator's overdeveloped prose; Bellow likes to inform us that his characters are "first-class noticers."

37

By the time the Flaubertian innovations have reached a novelist like Christopher Isherwood, writing in the 1930s, they have been polished to high technical shine. *Goodbye to Berlin*, published in 1939, has a famous early statement: "I am a camera with its shutter open, quite passive, recording, not thinking. Recording the man shaving at the window opposite and the woman in the kimono washing her hair. Some day, all this will have to be developed, carefully printed, fixed." Isherwood makes good on his claim in a scene-setting passage like this, from the opening of the chapter entitled "The Nowaks":

The entrance to the Wassertorstrasse was a big stone archway, a bit of old Berlin, daubed with hammers and sickles and Nazi crosses and plastered with tattered bills which advertised auctions or crimes. It was a deep shabby cobbled street, littered with sprawling children in tears. Youths in woollen sweaters circled waveringly across it on racing bikes and whooped at girls passing with milk-jugs. The pavement was chalk-marked for the hopping game

called Heaven and Earth. At the end of it, like a tall,
dangerously sharp, red instrument, stood a church.

Isherwood asserts even more flagrantly than
Flaubert a randomness of detail, while trying
even harder than Flaubert to disguise that randomness: this is exactly the formalization you
would expect of a literary style, once radical sev-
enty years ago, that is now decomposing a bit
into a familiar way of ordering reality on the
page—a set of handy rules, in effect. Posing as
a camera who simply records, Isherwood seems
merely to turn a wide bland gaze to the Wassertorstrasse: there, he says, is an archway, a street
littered with children, some youths on bikes and
girls with milk-jugs. Just a quick look. But, like
Flaubert, only much more assertively, Isherwood
insists on slowing down dynamic activity, and
freezing habitual occurrence. The street may
well be littered with children, but they cannot
all be "in tears" all the time. Likewise the cy-
cling youths and the walking milk girls, who are
presented as part of the habitual furniture of the
place. On the other hand, the tattered bills and
the ground marked with the children's game are
plucked by the author from their quiescence, and
made temporally noisy: they flash at us, suddenly, but they belong to a different time signa-
ture than the children and youths.

38

The more one looks at this rather wonderful piece of writing, the less it seems "a slice of life," or a camera's easy swipe, than a very careful ballet. The passage begins with an entrance: the entrance of the chapter. The reference to hammers and sickles and Nazi crosses introduces a note of menace, which is completed by the sardonic reference to commercial bills advertising "auctions or crimes": this may be commerce, but it is uncomfortably close to the political graffiti—after all, isn't auction and crime what politicians, especially the kind involved in communist or fascist activities, do? They sell us things and commit crimes. The Nazi "crosses" nicely link us to the children's game called Heaven and Earth, and to the church, except that, threateningly enough, everything is inverted: the church no longer looks like a church but like a red instrument (a pen, a knife, an instrument of torture, the "red" the color of both blood and radical politics), while the "cross" has been taken over by the Nazis. Given this inversion, we understand why Isherwood wants to top and tail this paragraph with the Nazi crosses at the start and the church at the end: each changes place in the course of a few lines.

39

So the narrator who promised that he was a mere camera, quite passive, recording, not thinking, is selling us a falsehood? Only in the sense that Robinson Crusoe's claim to be telling a true story is a falsehood: the reader is happy enough to efface the labor of the writer in order to believe two further fictions: that the narrator was somehow "really there" (and in fact Isherwood was living in Berlin in the 1930s), and that the narrator is not really a writer. Or rather, what Flaubert's flaneur tradition tries to establish is that the narrator (or designated authorial scout) *is at once a kind of writer and not really a writer.* A writer by temperament but not by trade. A writer because he notices so much, so well; not really a writer because he is not expending any labor to put it down on the page, and after all is really noticing no more than you and I would see.

This solution to the tension between the style of the author and the style of the character presents a paradox. It announces, in effect: "We moderns have all become writers, and all have highly sophisticated eyes for detail; but life is not actually as 'literary' as this implies, because we don't have to worry too much about how such detail gets onto the page." The tension between the style of the author and the style of the

character disappears because literary style itself is made to disappear: and literary style is
made to disappear through literary means.

40

Flaubertian realism, like most fiction, is both lifelike and artificial. It is lifelike because detail
really does hit us, especially in big cities, in a
tattoo of randomness. And we do exist in different time signatures. Suppose I am walking
down a street. I am aware of many noises, much
activity, a police siren, a building being de-
molished, the scrape of a shop door. Different
faces and bodies stream past me. And as I pass
a café, I catch the eye of a woman, who is sitting alone. She looks at me, I at her. A moment
of pointless, vaguely erotic urban connection,
but the face reminds me of someone I once knew,
a girl with just the same kind of dark hair, and
sets a train of thought going. I walk on, but that
particular face in the café glows in my memory,
is held there, and is being temporally preserved,
while around me noise and activities are not being similarly preserved—are entering and leaving my consciousness. The face, you could say, is
playing at 4/4, while the rest of the city is hum-
ming along more quickly at 6/8.

The artifice lies in the *selection* of detail. In life,

we can swivel our heads and eyes, but in fact we
are like helpless cameras. We have a wide lens,
and must take in whatever comes before us. Our
memory selects for us, but not much like the
way literary narrative selects. Our memories are
aesthetically untalented.

41

So realism is at once true and artificial, pulled
between life and art, the capacious and the se-
lective, the camera and the painting. And see
how vital these tensions still are, and what an
alert contemporary writer can do with them, in
Teju Cole's novel *Open City*. Cole's narrator, Julius, a young American intellectual, half-German
and half-Nigerian by birth, wanders around
New York City gathering impressions, hearing
stories, and floating his ideas. Julius is a twenty-
first-century flaneur, who has read Roland
Barthes and Edward Said and Kwame Anthony
Appiah—a good noticer and reader, an excep-
tional listener. Alert to his own mixed origins,
he seeks out people and stories that are neglected
or politically occluded: he talks to a Liberian refugee, a Haitian shoeshiner, an angry Moroccan
intellectual. He is compassionate, empathetic,
learned, liberal; almost our ideal sense of ourselves. But he also narrates his own story, and the

novel gradually reveals him to be an unreliable narrator. We begin to see that he isn't as empathetic as he thinks he is; he congratulates himself on the achievement of his liberalism, on the fineness of his noticing eye, while neglecting inconvenient or even grievous actions in his own life. Julius listens well to the story of a Liberian refugee, but he's rude to his African American cab driver; he seeks out a Moroccan intellectual in Belgium, but is complacently unaware that his neighbor's wife in New York died a few months ago.

Cole activates the tension in flaneurial realism between saturation and selection, and transfers it to the moral and political sphere. In the aesthetic or literary realm, the flaneurial tension is between what you helplessly record and what you choose to represent (between the cinematic and the painterly). In the moral or political realm, that tension manifests itself thus: what *should* we notice, and how much do we actually forget or neglect? And what do we then do about what we notice? It's all very well to listen to the Liberian refugee, but if I do nothing to help him or change his political circumstances, I am perhaps just a well-read flaneur, a morally idle Flaubertian. Maybe life, morally speaking, is just such a process of hapless noticing and neglect? And as readers of Cole's book, will we truly notice Julius's moral and political lapses, or will we neglect to see them? Will we read *Open City*, close it, and then do nothing about our own careless habits of witness? Will we become mere *flaneurs of the text itself*?

Detail

"But it's not possible any other way: only in the details can we understand the essential, as books and life have taught me. One needs to know every detail, since one can never be sure which of them is important, and which word shines out from behind things . . ."*

42

In 1985, the mountaineer Joe Simpson, twenty-one thousand feet up in the Andes, fell off an ice ledge and broke his leg. Dangling uselessly from his ropes, he was left for dead by his climbing partner. Into his head, unbidden, came the Boney M. song "Brown Girl in the Ring." He had never liked the song, and was infuriated at the thought of dying to this particular soundtrack.

In literature, as in life, death is often attended by apparent irrelevance, from Falstaff babbling of green fields, to Balzac's Lucien de Rubempré noticing architectural details just before taking his life (in *Splendeurs et misères des courtisanes*), to

---

*Sándor Márai, *Embers*, translated by Carol Brown Janeway (translation from the German version, 2001).

Prince Andrew on his deathbed dreaming of a trivial conversation in *War and Peace*, to Joachim in *The Magic Mountain* moving his arm along the blanket "as if he were collecting or gathering something." Proust implies that such irrelevance will always attend our deaths, because we are never prepared for them; we never think of our death as likely to occur "this very afternoon." Instead:

> One insists on one's daily outing so that in a month's time one will have had the necessary ration of fresh air; one has hesitated over which coat to take, which cabman to call; one is in the cab, the whole day lies before one, short because one must be back home early, as a friend is coming to see one; one hopes that it will be as fine again tomorrow; and one has no suspicion that death, which has been advancing within one on another plane, has chosen precisely this particular day to make its appearance, in a few minutes' time, more or less at the moment when the carriage reaches the Champs-Elysées.*

An example that comes close to Joe Simpson's experience occurs at the end of Chekhov's story "Ward 6." The doctor, Ragin, is dying: "A herd of deer, extraordinarily beautiful and graceful,

---

The Guermantes Way, Part 2, Chapter 1.

which he had read about the day before, ran past him; then a peasant woman reached out to him with a certified letter . . . Mikhail Averyanych said something. Then everything vanished and Andrei Yefimych lost consciousness forever." The peasant woman with the certified letter is a bit too "literary" (the grim reaper's summons, etc.); but that herd of deer!

How lovely the simplicity with which Chekhov, deep inside his character's mind, does not say, "He thought of the deer he had been reading about" or even "He saw in his mind the deer he had been reading about," but just calmly asserts that the deer "ran past him."

43

On March 28, 1941, Virginia Woolf loaded her pockets with stones and walked into the river Ouse. Her husband, Leonard Woolf, was obsessively punctilious, and had kept a journal every day of his adult life, in which he recorded daily menus and car mileage. Apparently, nothing was different on the day his wife committed suicide: he entered the mileage for his car. But on this day the paper is obscured by a smudge, writes his biographer, Victoria Glendinning, "a brownish-yellow stain which has been rubbed or wiped. It could be tea or coffee or tears. The smudge is unique in all his years of neat diary-keeping."

The fictional detail closest in spirit to Leonard Woolf's smudged journal describes the last hours of Thomas Buddenbrooks. Thomas's sister, Frau Permaneder, has been keeping a deathbed vigil. Passionate but stoical, she gives way at one moment to her grief, and sings a prayer: "Come, Lord, receive his failing breath." But she has forgotten that she does not know the whole verse, falters, "and had to make up for her abrupt end by the increased dignity of her manner." Everyone is embarrassed. Then Thomas dies and Frau Permaneder flings herself to the ground and weeps bitterly. A second later, control has been reasserted: "Her face still streamed with tears, but she was soothed and comforted and entirely herself as she rose to her feet and began straightway to occupy her mind with the announcement of the death—an enormous number of elegant cards, which must be ordered at once." Life returns to busyness and routine after the tearing of death. A commonplace. But the selection of that adjective "elegant" is subtle; the bourgeois order stirs to life with its "elegant" cards, and Mann suggests that this class retains faith in the solidity and grace of objects, clings to them indeed.

44

In 1960, during the presidential campaign, Richard Nixon and John F. Kennedy fought the first-ever televised debate. It is often said that the sweating Nixon "lost" because he had a five o'clock shadow, and looked sinister.

People thought they knew what Richard Nixon looked like, until he was placed alongside the fairer Kennedy, and the television lights blazed. Then he looked different. Likewise, the married Anna Karenina meets Vronsky on the night train from Moscow to Petersburg. By morning, something important has changed, but is as yet not properly acknowledged by her. To evoke this, Tolstoy has Anna notice her husband, Karenin, in a new light. Karenin has come to meet Anna at the station, and the first thing she thinks is: "Oh, mercy! Why have his ears become like that?" Her husband looks cold and imposing, but above all it is the ears that suddenly seem strange—"his ears whose cartilages propped up the brim of his round hat of black felt."

45

Boney M., the single smudge, Nixon's shadow: in life as in literature, we navigate via the stars of detail. We use detail to focus, to fix an impression, to recall. We snag on it. In Isaac Babel's story "My First Fee," a teenage boy is telling a prostitute a tall tale. She is bored and skeptical, until he says, fancifully, that he took "bronze promissory notes" to a woman. Suddenly, she is hooked.

46

Literature differs from life in that life is amorphously full of detail, and rarely directs us toward it, whereas literature teaches us to notice—to notice the way my mother, say, often wipes her lips just before kissing me; the drilling sound of a London cab when its diesel engine is flabbily idling; the way old leather jackets have white lines in them like the striations of fat in pieces of meat; the way fresh snow "creaks" underfoot; the way a baby's arms are so fat that they seem tied with string (the others are mine but that last example is from Tolstoy.).*

---

*It is from *Anna Karenina*, and is a nice example of self-plagiarism. In that novel, not one but two babies—Levin's and Anna's—are described as looking as if string is tied around their fat little arms. Likewise, in *David Copperfield*, Dickens likens Uriah Heep's open mouth to a post office, and Wemmick's open mouth, in *Great Expectations*—to a post office. Stendhal writes, in *The Red and the Black*, about how politics ruins a novel in the way a gunshot would spoil a music concert, and then repeats the image in *The Charterhouse of Parma*. Henry James wrote that Balzac, in his monkish devotion to his art, was "a Benedictine of the actual," a phrase he liked so much he used it later about Flaubert. Cormac

47

This tutoring is dialectical. Literature makes us better noticers of life; we get to practice on life itself; which in turn makes us better readers of detail in literature; which in turn makes us better readers of life. And so on and on. You have only to teach literature to realize that most young readers are poor noticers. I know from my own old books, wantonly annotated twenty years ago when I was a student, that I routinely underlined for approval details and images and metaphors that strike me now as commonplace, while serenely missing things that now seem wonderful. We grow, as readers, and twenty-year-olds are relative virgins. They have not yet read enough literature to be taught by it how to read it.

48

Writers can be like those twenty-year-olds, too—stuck at different floors of visual talent. As in all departments of aesthetics, there are levels

---

McCarthy writes, in *Blood Meridian*, "the blue cordilleras stood footed in their paler image on the sand," and returns to that lovely verb seven years later in *All the Pretty Horses*: "Where a pair of herons stood footed to their long shadows." Why shouldn't he? Such things are rarely examples of haste and more often proof that a style has achieved self-consistency. And that a kind of Platonic ideal has been reached—these are the best, and therefore unsurpassable words, for these subjects.

of success in noticing. Some writers are modestly endowed noticers, others are stupendously observant. And there are plenty of moments in fiction when a writer seems to hold back, keeping a power in reserve: an ordinary observation is followed by a remarkable detail, a spectacular enrichment of observation, as if the writer had been, previously, just warming up, with the prose now suddenly opening like a daylily.

49

How would we know when a detail seems really true? What guides us? The medieval theologian Duns Scotus gave the name "thisness" (*haecceitas*) to individuating form. The idea was adapted by Gerard Manley Hopkins, whose poetry and prose is full of thisness: the "lovely behaviour" of "silk-sack clouds" ("Hurrahing in Harvest"); or "the glassy peartree" whose leaves "brush / The descending blue; that blue is all in a rush / With richness . . ." ("Spring").

Thisness is a good place to start.

By thisness, I mean any detail that draws abstraction toward itself and seems to kill that abstraction with a puff of palpability, any detail that centers our attention with its concretion. Marlow, in *Heart of Darkness*, recalls a man dying at his feet, with a spear in his stomach, and how "my feet felt so very warm and wet that I had to look down . . . my shoes were full; a pool of blood lay very still, gleaming dark-red under the wheel."* The man lies on his back, looking up at Marlow anxiously, gripping the spear in his stomach as if it were "something precious, with an air of being afraid I would try to take it away from him." By thisness, I mean the kind of exact palpabilities that Pushkin squeezes into the fourteen-line stanzas of *Eugene Onegin*: Eugene's country estate, for instance, which has not been touched for years, where the unopened cupboards contain fruit liqueurs, "a book of household calculations," and an obsolete "calendar for 1808," and where the billiards table is equipped with a "blunt cue."

By thisness, I mean the precise brand of greenness—"Kendal green"—that Falstaff swears, in *Henry IV, Part 1*, clothed the men who attacked him: "three misbegotten knaves in Kendal green came at my back and let drive at me." There is something wonderfully absurd about "Kendal green": it sounds as if the ambushing "knaves" did not just jump out from behind bushes, but were somehow dressed *as* bushes! And Falstaff is lying.

---

*The image was heavily borrowed by Cormac McCarthy in *No Country for Old Men* (2005), where people are forever having their boots fill up with blood—usually their own, however.

He saw no men dressed in Kendal green; it was too dark. The comedy of the specificity—already perhaps inherent in the very name—is doubled because it is a fiction posing as a specificity; and Hal, aware of this, presses Falstaff, reiterating the ridiculous precision: "Why, how couldst thou know these men in Kendal green, when it was so dark thou couldst not see thy hand?"

By thisness, I mean the moment when Emma Bovary fondles the satin slippers she danced in weeks before at the great ball at La Vaubyessard, "the soles of which were yellowed with the wax from the dance floor." By thisness, I mean the cow manure that Ajax slips in while racing at the grand funeral games, in Book 23 of *The Iliad* (thisness is often used to puncture ceremonies like funerals and dinners that are designed precisely to euphemize thisness: what Tolstoy calls making a bad smell in the drawing room).* By thisness, I mean the single "cherry-coloured twist" that the tailor of Gloucester, in Beatrix Potter's tale of the same name, has not yet sewn. (Reading this to my daughter recently, for the first time in thirty-five years, I was instantly returned, by the talismanic activity of that "cherry-coloured twist," to a memory

---

*From *The Death of Ivan Ilyich*; Tolstoy likens talking about death, which polite society must ignore, to someone making a bad smell in a drawing room.

of my mother reading it to me. Beatrix Potter means the red satin that must be sewn around the eyelet of a buttonhole on a fancy coat. But perhaps the phrase was so magical to me then because it sounded so sweet: like a licorice or sherbet *twist*—a word that was still used, then, by confectioners.)

50

Because thisness is palpability, it will tend toward substance—cow shit, red silk, the wax of a ballroom floor, a calendar for 1808, blood in a boot. But it can be a mere name or an anecdote; palpability can be represented in the form of an anecdote or a piquant fact. In *A Portrait of the Artist as a Young Man*, Stephen Dedalus sees that Mr. Casey's fingers can't be straightened out, "and Mr. Casey had told him that he had got those three cramped fingers making a birthday present for Queen Victoria." Why is this detail, about making a birthday present for Queen Victoria, so alive? We begin with the comic specificity, the concrete allusion: if Joyce had written only "and Mr. Casey got cramped fingers making a birthday present," the detail would obviously be relatively flat, relatively vague. If he had written: "and he got those *three* cramped fingers making a birthday present for *Aunt Mary*," the details would be

livelier, but why? Is specificity in itself satisfy-
ing? I think it is, and we expect such satisfaction from literature. We want names and
numbers.* And the source of the comedy and
liveliness here lies in a nice paradox of expectation and its denial: the sentence has insufficient
detail in one area and overspecific detail in another. It is clearly inadequate to claim that
Mr. Casey got his permanently cramped fingers
from making "a birthday present": What titanic
operation could possibly have crippled him like
this? So our hunger for specificity is excited by
this comic vagueness; and then Joyce deliberately
feeds us too much specificity with the detail
about the recipient. It is gratifying to have been
given so much fact, but the fact about Queen
Victoria, posing as specific, is really very mysterious, and flagrantly fails to answer the basic
question: What was the present? (There is a
deeper political secret: making a present for
Queen Victoria means that Mr. Casey, a radical,

---

*Lawrence's story "Odour of Chrysanthemums" begins like this: "The
small locomotive engine, Number 4, came clanking, stumbling down
from Selston—with seven full wagons." Ford Madox Ford, who published it in the *English Review* in 1911, said that the precision of the
"Number 4" and the "seven" wagons announced the presence of a real
writer. "The ordinary careless writer," he said, "would say 'some small
wagons.' This man knows what he wants. He sees the scene of his story
exactly." See John Worthen's biography *D. H. Lawrence: The Early Years,
1885-1912* (1991).

has been in prison.) Joyce's sentence is thus made up of two mysterious details—the gift and its recipient—with the latter posing as the answer to the former mystery. The comedy is all to do with our desire for thisness in detail, and Joyce's determination to merely *pretend* to satisfy it. Queen Victoria, like Falstaff's fictional Kendal green, is represented as the detail that promises to illuminate the surrounding gloom; or, we might say, the fact that promises to ground the fiction. It *does* ground the fiction, in one sense: our attention is surely drawn to the concretion. But in another sense, it is funny because it either is (like Kendal green) or seems (Queen Victoria) more fictional than the surrounding fiction.

51

I confess to an ambivalence about detail in fiction. I relish it, consume it, ponder it. Hardly a day goes by in which I don't remind myself of Bellow's description of Mr. Rappaport's cigar: "the white ghost of the leaf with all its veins and its fainter pungency." But I choke on too much detail, and find that a distinctively post-Flaubertian tradition fetishizes it: the overaesthetic appreciation of detail seems to raise, in a slightly different form, that tension between author and character we have already explored.

If the history of the novel can be told as the development of free indirect style, it can no less be told as the rise of detail. It is hard to recall for how long fictional narrative was in thrall to neoclassical ideals, which favored the formulaic and the imitative rather than the individual and the original.* Of course, original and individual detail can never be suppressed: Pope and Defoe and even Fielding are full of what Blake called the "minute particulars." But it is impossible to imagine a novelist in 1770 saying what Flaubert said to Maupassant in 1870: "There is a part of everything which is unexplored, because we are accustomed to using our eyes only in association with the memory of what people before us have thought of the thing we are looking at. Even the smallest thing has something in it which is unknown."† J. M. Coetzee, in his novel *Elizabeth Costello*, has this to say about Defoe:

---

*A nice index of this can be found in Adam Smith's *Lectures on Rhetoric and Belles Lettres* (1762–63), in which he says that poetic and rhetorical description should be brief, to the point, and not lengthy. But, he goes on, "it is often proper to Choose out some nice and Curious" detail. "A Painter in Drawing a fruit makes the figure very striking if he not only gives it the form and Colour but also represents the fine down with which it is covered." Smith recommends this in such a fresh and ingenuous way—as if he is saying, "Wouldn't it be a good idea to notice the fine down on a piece of fruit?"—that he makes the very concept of detail sound somewhat novel and newfangled.

†Maupassant, "The Novel," preface to *Pierre and Jean* (1888).

The blue costume, the greasy hair, are details, signs of a moderate realism. Supply the particulars, allow the significations to emerge of themselves. A procedure pioneered by Daniel Defoe. Robinson Crusoe, cast up upon the beach, looks around for his shipmates. But there are none. "I never saw them afterwards, or any sign of them," says he, "except three of their hats, one cap, and two shoes that were not fellows." Two shoes, not fellows: by not being fellows, the shoes have ceased to be footwear and become proofs of death, torn by the foaming seas off the feet of drowning men and tossed ashore. No large words, no despair, just hats and caps and shoes.

Coetzee's phrase "moderate realism" describes a way of writing in which the kind of detail we are directed to does not yet have the kind of extravagant commitment to noticing and renoticing, to novelty and strangeness, characteristic of modern novelists—an eighteenth-century regime, in which the cult of "detail" has not yet really been established.

52

You can read *Don Quixote* or *Tom Jones* or Austen's novels and find very little of the detail Flaubert recommends. Austen gives us none of the visual furniture we find in Balzac or Joyce, and hardly ever stops to describe even a character's face. Clothes, climates, interiors, all are elegantly compressed and thinned. Minor characters in Cervantes, Fielding, and Austen are theatrical, often formulaic, and are barely noticed, *in a visual sense*. Fielding quite happily describes two different characters in *Joseph Andrews* as having "Roman noses."

But for Flaubert, for Dickens, and for hundreds of novelists after them, the minor character is a delicious kind of stylistic challenge: How to make us see him, how to animate him, how to dab him with a little gloss? (Like Dora's cousin in *David Copperfield*, who is "in the Life-Guards, with such long legs that he looked like the afternoon shadow of somebody else.") Here is Flaubert's sidelong glance at a minor character at a ball, never seen again, in *Madame Bovary*:

> There, at the top of the table, alone among all these women, stooped over his ample plateful, with his napkin tied around his neck like a child, an old man sat eating, drops of gravy dribbling from his lips. His eyes were bloodshot and he had a little pigtail tied up with a black ribbon. This was the Marquis's father-in-law, the old Duc de Laverdière, once the favourite of the Comte d'Artois . . . and he, so they said, had been the lover of Marie Antoinette, in between Monsieurs de Coigny and de Lauzun. He had

led a tumultuous life of debauchery and dueling, of
wagers made and women abducted, had squandered
his fortune and terrified his whole family.

As so often, the Flaubertian legacy is a mixed
blessing. Again, there is the tiresome burden of
"chosenness" we feel around Flaubert's details,
and the implication of that chosenness for the
novelist's characters—our sense that the selection of detail has become a poet's obsessive
excruciation rather than a novelist's easy joy.
(The flaneur—the hero who is both a writer and
not a writer—solves this problem, or attempts
to. But in the example above, Flaubert has no
adequate surrogate, because his surrogate is
Emma: so in effect this is the novelist, pure and
simple, watching.) Here is Rilke, in *The Notebooks
of Malte Laurids Brigge*, being excruciatingly exact about a blind man he has seen in the street:
"I had undertaken the task of imagining him,
and was sweating from the effort . . . I understood that nothing about him was insignificant . . . his hat, an old, high-crowned, stiff felt
hat, which he wore the way all blind men wear
their hats: without any relation to the lines of the
face, without the possibility of adding this feature to themselves and forming a new external
unity: but merely as an arbitrary, extraneous
object." Impossible to imagine a writer before

Flaubert indulging in these theatrics ("was sweating from the effort")! What Rilke says about the blind man reads like a projection of his own sweaty literary anxieties onto the man: when no literary detail is insignificant, then perhaps each will indeed fail to "form a new external unity" and will be "merely" an "arbitrary, extraneous object."

In Flaubert and his successors we have the sense that the ideal of writing is a procession of strung details, a necklace of noticings, and that this is sometimes an obstruction to seeing, not an aid.

53

So during the nineteenth century, the novel became more *painterly*. In *La Peau de chagrin*, Balzac describes a tablecloth "white as a layer of newly fallen snow, upon which the place-settings rise symmetrically, crowned with blond rolls." Cézanne said that all through his youth he "wanted to paint that, that tablecloth of new snow."* Nabokov and Updike at times freeze detail into a cult of itself. Aestheticism is the

---

*Quoted in Maurice Merleau-Ponty, "Cézanne's Doubt," in *Sense and Non-Sense* (1948), translated by Hubert L. Dreyfus and Patricia Allen Dreyfus (1964).

great risk here, and also an exaggeration of the noticing eye. (There is so much detail in life that is not purely visual.) The Nabokov who writes, "an elderly flower girl, with carbon eyebrows and a painted smile, nimbly slipped the plump torus of a carnation into the buttonhole of an intercepted stroller whose left jowl accentuated its royal fold as he glanced down sideways at the coy insertion of the flower," becomes the Updike who notices the rain on a window thus: "Its panes were strewn with drops that as if by amoebic decision would abruptly merge and break and jerkily run downward, and the window screen, like a sampler half-stitched, or a crossword puzzle invisibly solved, was inlaid erratically with minute, translucent tesserae of rain."* It is significant that Updike likens the rainy window to a crossword puzzle: both these writers, in this mode, sound as if they are setting us a puzzle.

Bellow notices superbly; but Nabokov wants to tell us how important it is to notice. Nabokov's fiction is always becoming propaganda on behalf of good noticing, hence on behalf of itself. There are beauties that are not visual at all,

---

*From Nabokov, "First Love" (1925) and Updike, *Of the Farm* (1961). And one can hear how David Foster Wallace comes out of this tradition, too, even if he renders comically or ironically a level of obsessive detail that Updike renders more earnestly.

and Nabokov has poorish eyes for those. How else to explain his dismissals of Mann, Camus, Faulkner, Stendhal, James? He judges them, essentially, for not being stylish enough, and for not being visually alert enough. The battle line emerges clearly in one of his exchanges with the critic Edmund Wilson, who had been trying to get Nabokov to read Henry James. At last, Nabokov cast his eye over *The Aspern Papers*, but reported back to Wilson that James was sloppy with detail. When James describes the lit end of a cigar, seen from outside a window, he calls it a "red tip." But cigars don't have tips, says Nabokov. James wasn't *looking* hard enough. He goes on to compare James's writing to "the weak blond prose" of Turgenev.*

A cigar, again! Here are two different approaches to the creation of detail. James, I think, would reply that first of all, cigars do have tips, and second, that there is no need, every time one describes a cigar, to do a Bellovian or Nabokovian job on it. That James was *incapable* of doing such a job—the implication of Nabokov's complaint—is easily disproved. But James is certainly not a Nabokovian writer; his notion of what constitutes a detail is more various, more impalpable, and finally more metaphysical than

The Nabokov-Wilson Letters, edited by Simon Karlinsky (1979).

Nabokov's. James would probably argue that while we should indeed try to be the kind of writer on whom nothing is lost, we have no need to be the kind of writer on whom everything is found.

54

There is a conventional modern fondness for quiet but "telling" detail: "The detective noticed that Carla's hairband was surprisingly dirty." If there is such a thing as a telling detail, then there must be such a thing as an untelling detail, no? A better distinction might be between what I would call "off-duty" and "on-duty" detail; the off-duty detail is part of the standing army of life, as it were—it is always ready to be activated. Literature is full of such off-duty detail (James's red cigar tip would be an example).

But maybe "off-duty" and "on-duty" just rephrases the problem? Isn't off-duty detail essentially detail that is not as telling as its on-duty comrades? Nineteenth-century realism, from Balzac on, creates such an abundance of detail that the modern reader has come to expect of narrative that it will always contain a certain superfluity, a built-in redundancy, that it will *carry more detail than it needs*. In other words, fiction builds into itself a lot of surplus detail just as life is full of surplus detail. Suppose I were to describe a man's head like this: "He had very red skin, and his eyes were bloodshot; his brow looked angry. There was a small mole on his upper lip." The red skin and bloodshot eyes and angry skin tell us, perhaps, something about the man's disposition, but the mole seems "irrelevant." It's just "there"; it is reality, it is just "how he looked."

55

But is this layer of gratuitous detail actually like life or just a trick? In his essay "The Reality Effect,"* Roland Barthes essentially argues that "irrelevant" detail is a code we no longer notice, and one that has little to do with how life really is. He discusses a passage by the historian Jules Michelet, in which Michelet is describing the last hours of Charlotte Corday in prison. An artist visits her and paints her portrait, and then "after an hour and a half, there was a gentle knock at a little door behind her." Then Barthes turns to Flaubert's description of Mme Aubain's room in *A Simple Heart*: "Eight mahogany chairs were lined up against the white-painted wain-

---

*Collected in *The Rustle of Language*, translated by Richard Howard (1986).

scoting, and under the barometer stood an old piano loaded with a pyramid of boxes and cartons." The piano, Barthes argues, is there to suggest bourgeois status, the boxes and cartons perhaps to suggest disorder. But why is the barometer there? The barometer denotes nothing; it is an object "neither incongruous nor significant"; it is apparently "irrelevant." Its business is to denote reality, it is there to create the effect, the atmosphere of the real. It simply says: "I am the real." (Or if you prefer: "I am realism.")

An object like the barometer, Barthes continues, is *supposed* to denote the real, but in fact all it does is signify it. In the Michelet passage, the little "filler" of the knock at the door is the kind of thing that this writing "puts in" to create the realistic "effect" of time passing. Realism in general, it is implied, is just such a business of false denotation. The barometer is interchangeable with a hundred other items; realism is an artificial tissue of mere arbitrary signs. Realism offers the appearance of reality but is in fact utterly fake—what Barthes calls "the referential illusion."

In *Mythologies*, Barthes wittily pointed out that those laurel-leaf haircuts worn by the actors in Hollywood's "Roman" films signify "Romanness" in the way that Flaubert's barometer signifies "realness." In neither case is anything

actually *real* being denoted. These are mere stylistic conventions, in the way that flares or the
miniskirt have meaning only as part of a system
of signification established by the fashion indus-
try itself. The codes of fashion are entirely arbitrary. As far as he was concerned, literature was
like fashion, because both systems make one
read the signifying of things rather than their
meaning.*

56

Isn't Barthes too quick to decide what is relevant
and irrelevant detail? Why is the barometer irrelevant? If the barometer exists only to arbi-
trarily proclaim the real, why don't the piano
and boxes, too? As A. D. Nuttall puts it in *A
New Mimesis*, the barometer doesn't say "I am the
real" so much as "Am I not just the sort of thing
you would find in such a house?" It is neither
incongruous nor especially significant, precisely
because it is dully typical. There are plenty of
houses that still have such barometers, and those
barometers indeed tell us something about the
kinds of houses they are in: middle class rather
than upper class; a certain kind of convention-
ality; a musty devotion, perhaps, to second-rate

Système de la mode (1967).

heirlooms; and the barometer is *never right*, is it? What does this tell us? In Britain, of course, they are especially comical tools, since the weather is always the same: gray, a bit of rain. You would never need a barometer. In fact, barometers, you might say, are very good barometers of a certain middling status: barometers are very good barometers of themselves! (*That's* how they work, then.)

Anyway, one can accept Barthes's stylistic proviso without accepting his epistemological caveat: fictional reality is indeed made up of such "effects," but realism can be an effect and still be true. It is only Barthes's sensitive, murderous hostility to realism that insists on this false division.

57

In Orwell's essay "A Hanging," the writer watches the condemned man, walking toward the gallows, swerve to avoid a puddle. For Orwell, this represents precisely what he calls the "mystery" of the life that is about to be taken: when there is no good reason for it, the condemned man is still thinking about keeping his shoes clean. It is an "irrelevant" act (and a marvelous bit of noticing on Orwell's part). Now suppose this were not an essay but a piece of fic-

tion. And indeed there has been a fair amount
of speculation about the proportion of fact to fiction in such essays of Orwell's. The avoidance of
the puddle would be precisely the kind of superb
detail that, say, Tolstoy might flourish; *War and
Peace* has an execution scene very close in spirit
to Orwell's essay, and it may well be that Orwell basically cribbed the detail from Tolstoy. In
War and Peace, Pierre witnesses a man being executed by the French, and notices that, just before death, the man adjusts the blindfold at the
back of his head, because it is uncomfortably
tight.* The avoidance of the puddle, the fiddling
with the blindfold—these are what might be
called irrelevant or superfluous details. They are
not explicable; in fiction, they exist to denote
precisely the inexplicable. This is one of the "effects" of realism, of "realistic" style. But Orwell's
essay, assuming it records an actual occurrence,
shows us that such fictional effects are not merely
conventionally irrelevant, or formally arbitrary,
but have something to tell us about the *irrelevance of reality itself*. In other words, the category
of the irrelevant or inexplicable exists in life, just
as the barometer exists, in all its uselessness, in
real houses. There was no logical reason for the
condemned man to avoid the puddle. It was pure

---

*Book Four, Chapter 11.

remembered habit. Life, then, will always contain an inevitable surplus, a margin of the gratuitous, a realm in which there is always more than we need: more things, more impressions, more memories, more habits, more words, more happiness, more unhappiness.

58

The barometer, the puddle, the adjustment of the blindfold, are not "irrelevant"; they are significantly insignificant. In "The Lady with the Little Dog," a man and a woman go to bed. After sex, the man calmly eats a melon: "There was a watermelon on the table in the hotel room. Gurov cut himself a slice and unhurriedly began to eat it. At least half an hour passed in silence." That is all Chekhov writes. He could have done it like this: "Thirty minutes passed. Outside, a dog started barking, and some children ran down the street. The hotel manager yelled something. A door slammed." These details would obviously be exchangeable with other, similar details; they are not crucial to anything. They would be there to make us feel that this is lifelike. Their insignificance is precisely their significance. And, as in the Michelet passage of which Barthes is so suspicious, one of the obvious reasons for the rise of this kind of significantly insignificant detail is that it is needed to evoke the passage of time, and fiction has a new and unique project in literature—the management of temporality. In ancient narratives, for instance, like Plutarch's *Lives* or the Bible stories, gratuitous detail is very hard to find. Mostly detail is functional or symbolic. Likewise, the ancient storytellers seem to feel no pressure to evoke a lifelike passing of "real time" (Chekhov's thirty minutes). Time passes jerkily, swiftly: "And Abraham rose up early in the morning, and saddled his ass, and took two of his young men with him, and Isaac his son, and clave the wood for the burnt offering, and rose up, and went unto the place of which God had told him. Then on the third day Abraham lifted up his eyes, and saw the place afar off." Time lapses *between* the verses, invisibly, inaudibly, but nowhere on the page. Each new "and" or "then" moves forward the action like those old station clocks, whose big hands suddenly slip forward once a minute.

We have seen that Flaubert's method of different temporalities requires a combination of details, some of which are relevant, some studiedly irrelevant. "*Studiedly* irrelevant"—we concede that there really is no such thing as irrelevant detail in fiction, even in realism, which tends to use such detail as a kind of padding, to make verisimilitude seem nice and comfy. You wastefully leave lights on in your home or hotel room when you aren't there, not to prove that you exist, but because *the margin of surplus itself* feels like life, feels in some curious way like being alive.

59

In "The Dead," Joyce writes that Gabriel was his old aunts' favorite nephew: "He was their favourite nephew, the son of their dead elder sister, Ellen, who had married T. J. Conroy of the Port and Docks." This might not look like anything much, at first; perhaps one has to be familiar with a certain kind of petit bourgeois snobbery to appreciate it. But what a lot it tells us about the two sisters, in just a handful of words! It is the kind of detail that speeds on our knowledge of a character: a state of mind, a gesture, a stray word. It pertains to human and moral understanding—detail not as thisness but as knowledge.

Joyce drops into free indirect style at the very end of the sentence, to inhabit the collective mind of the proper and snobbish old ladies, who are "caught" thinking about their brother-in-law's status. Imagine if the line went: "He was their favourite nephew, Ellen and Tom's fine son."

The sentence would tell us nothing about the sisters. Instead, Joyce's point is that *inside their own minds, in their private voices,* they still think of their brother-in-law not as "Tom," but as "T. J. Conroy of the Port and Docks." They are proud of his attainment, of his substance in the world, even a little daunted by it. And that gnomic "of the Port and Docks" functions like the birthday present for Queen Victoria: we don't know what T. J. Conroy did at the Port and Docks, and it is exquisitely difficult to know how grand a job at the Port and Docks could possibly be. (That is the comedy.) But Joyce—working in a manner exactly opposite to Updike in that passage from *Terrorist*—knows that to tell us any more about the Port and Docks would ruin the psychological truth: *this* status means something important to *these* women. It is enough to know that.

This sudden capturing of a central human truth, this moment when a single detail has suddenly enabled us to see a character's thinking (or lack of it), can be a branch of free indirect style, as in the example above. But not necessarily: it may be the novelist's observation from "outside" the character (though it speeds us inside, of course). There is such a moment in *The Radetzky March,* when the old captain visits his dying servant, who is in bed, and the servant

tries to click his naked heels together under the
sheets . . . or in *The Possessed*, when the proud,
weak governor, von Lembke, loses his control.
Shouting at a group of visitors in his drawing
room, he marches out, only to trip on the carpet. Standing still, he looks at the carpet and
ridiculously yells, "Have it changed!"—and
walks out . . . or when Charles Bovary returns
with his wife from the grand ball at La Vaubyessard, which has so enchanted Emma, rubs his
hands together, and says: "It's good to be
home" . . . or in *Sentimental Education*, when Frédéric takes his rather humble mistress to Fon-
tainebleau. She is bored, but can tell that Frédéric
is frustrated with her lack of culture. So in one
of the galleries, she looks around at the paintings, and, trying to say something knowing and
impressive, merely exclaims: "All this brings
back memories!" . . . or when, after his divorce,
Anna Karenina's husband, the stiff and joyless
civil servant, goes around introducing himself
with the line: "You are acquainted with my
grief?"

60

These details help us to "know" Karenin or
Bovary or Frédéric's mistress, but they also present a mystery. Years ago, my wife and I were at

a concert given by the violinist Nadja Salerno-Sonnenberg. At a quiet, difficult passage of bowing, she frowned. Not the usual ecstatic moue of the virtuoso, it expressed sudden irritation. At the same moment, we invented entirely different readings. Claire later said to me: "She was frowning because she wasn't playing that bit well enough." I replied: "I think she was frowning because the audience was so noisy." A good novelist would have let that frown alone, and would have let our revealing comments alone, too: no need to smother this little scene in explanation.

Detail like this—that enters a character but refuses to explain that character—makes us the writer as well as the reader; we seem like co-creators of the character's existence. We have an *idea* of what is going through von Lembke's mind when he shouts, "Have it changed!" but there are several possible readings; we have an idea of Rosanette's awkwardness, but we can't know what exactly she means when she says, "All this brings back memories!" These characters are somehow very private, even as they artlessly expose themselves.*

"The Lady with the Little Dog" is almost

---

*"A shot can be a word, but it's better when it's a sentence," says Francis Ford Coppola in *Live Cinema and Its Techniques* (2017). He means that details are stronger when complex and enigmatic.

entirely composed of details that refuse to explain themselves, and this suits the story because it is about a love affair that brings a great happiness somewhat inexplicable to the lovers. A married man—and expert seducer—meets a married woman in Yalta; they go to bed. Why do at least thirty minutes go by in silence as Gurov eats his melon? Several reasons come to mind: and we fill that silence with *our* reasons. Later in the story, the confident seducer decides, in ways he cannot fully express, that this ordinary-looking woman from a small town means more to him than anyone he has ever loved. He journeys from Moscow to the woman's provincial town, and they meet at the local theater. The orchestra, writes Chekhov, takes *a long time to tune*. (Again, no commentary is offered: we are free to assume that provincial orchestras are inexpert.) The lovers snatch a moment outside the auditorium, on the stairs. Above, two schoolboys watch them, smoking. Do the boys know what drama is happening beneath them? Are they indifferent? Are the lovers troubled by the surveillance of the schoolboys? Chekhov does not say.

The perfection of the detail has to do with symmetry: two malefactors have encountered two other malefactors, and each couple has nothing to do with the other.

Character

The punchline of the story relates to an American aca-demic saying of Beckett, "He doesn't give a fuck about people. He's an artist." At this point Beckett raised his voice above the clatter of afternoon tea and shouted, "But I do give a fuck about people! I do give a fuck!"*

61

There is nothing harder than the creation of fic-tional character. I can tell it from the number of apprentice novels I read that begin with de-scriptions of photographs. You know the style: "My mother is squinting in the fierce sunlight and holding, for some reason, a dead pheasant. She is dressed in old-fashioned lace-up boots, and white gloves. She looks absolutely misera-ble. My father, however, is in his element, irre-pressible as ever, and has on his head that gray velvet trilby from Prague I remember so well from my childhood." The unpracticed novelist cleaves to the static, because it is much easier to

---

* *Beckett Remembering, Remembering Beckett*, edited by James and Eliza-beth Knowlson (2006).

describe than the mobile: it is getting these
people out of the aspic of arrest and mobilized
in a scene that is hard. When I encounter a pro-
longed ekphrasis like the parody above, I worry,
suspecting that the novelist is clinging to a
handrail and is afraid to push out.

62

But how to push out? How to animate the static
portrait? Ford Madox Ford, in his book *Joseph
Conrad: A Personal Remembrance*, writes wonderfully about getting a character up and
running—what he calls "getting a character *in*."
He says that Conrad himself "was never really
satisfied that he had really and sufficiently got
his characters in; he was never convinced that he
had convinced the reader; this accounting for the
great lengths of some of his books." I like this
idea, that some of Conrad's novels are long
because he couldn't stop fiddling, page after
page, with the verisimilitude of his characters—
it raises the specter of an infinite novel. At least
the apprentice writer, with his bundle of nerves,
is in good company, then. Ford and Conrad
loved a sentence from a Maupassant story, "La
Reine Hortense": "He was a gentleman with red
whiskers who always went first through a door-
way." Ford comments: "That gentleman is so

sufficiently got in that you need no more of him to understand how he will act. He has been 'got in' and can get to work at once."

Ford is right. Very few brushstrokes are needed to get a portrait walking, as it were; and—a corollary of this—that the reader can get as much from small, short-lived, even rather flat characters as from large, round, towering heroes and heroines. To my mind, Gurov, the adulterer in "The Lady with the Little Dog," is as vivid, as rich, and as sustaining as Gatsby or Dreiser's Hurstwood, or even Jane Eyre.

63

Let us think about this for a moment. A stranger enters a room. How do we immediately begin to take his measure? We look at his face, his clothing, for sure. This man, let us say, is middle-aged, still handsome, but going bald—he has a smooth space on the top of his head, fringed with flattened hair, which looks like a pale crop circle. Something about his carriage suggests a man who expects to be noticed; on the other hand, he smooths his hand over his head so often in the first few minutes that one suspects him of being a little uneasy about having lost that hair.

This man, let us say, is curious, because the

top half of him is expensively turned out—a fine, pressed shirt, a good jacket—while the bottom half is slovenly: stained, creased trousers, old unpolished shoes. Does he expect, then, that people will only notice the top of him? Might this suggest a certain faith in his own theatrical ability to hold people's attention? (Keep them looking at your face.) Or perhaps his own life is similarly bifurcated? Perhaps he is ordered in some ways, disordered in others.

64

In Antonioni's film *L'Eclisse*, the luminous Monica Vitti visits the Rome stock exchange, where her fiancé, played by Alain Delon, works. Delon points out a fat man who has just lost 50 million lire. Intrigued, she follows the man. He orders a drink at a bar, barely touches it, then goes to a café, where he orders an *acqua minerale*, which he again barely touches. He is writing something on a piece of paper, and leaves it on the table. We imagine that it must be a set of furious, melancholy figures. Vitti approaches the table, and sees that it is a drawing of a flower . . .

Who would not love this little scene? It is so delicate, so tender, so sidelong and lightly humorous, and the joke is so nicely on us. We had a stock idea of how the financial victim responds to catastrophe—collapse, despair, self-defenestration—and Antonioni confounded our expectations. The character slips through our changing perceptions, like a boat moving through canal locks. We begin in misplaced certainty and end in placeless mystery.

The scene raises the question of what really constitutes a character. We know nothing more about this investor than this scene tells us; he has no continuing role in the film. Is he really a "character" at all? Yet no one would dispute that Antonioni has revealed something sharp and deep about this man's temperament, and by extension about a certain human insouciance under pressure—or possibly, about a certain defensive will to insouciance under pressure. Something alive, human has been disclosed. So this scene demonstrates that narrative can and often does give us a vivid sense of a character without giving us a vivid sense of an individual. We don't know this particular man; but we know his particular behavior at this moment.

65

A great deal of nonsense is written every day about characters in fiction—from the side of those who believe too much in character and from the side of those who believe too little.

Those who believe too much have an iron set of
prejudices about what characters are: we should
get to "know" them; they should not be "stereo-
types"; they should have an "inside" as well as
an outside, depth as well as surface; they should
"grow" and "develop"; and they should be nice.
So they should be pretty much like us.

66

On the other side, among those with too little
belief in character, we hear that characters do not
exist at all. The brilliant novelist and critic
William Gass comments on the following passage from Henry James's *The Awkward Age*:
"Mr. Cashmore, who would have been very
red-haired if he had not been very bald, showed
a single eye-glass and a long upper lip; he was
large and jaunty, with little petulant movements
and intense ejaculations that were not in the line
of his type." Of this, Gass says:

> We can imagine any number of other sentences
> about Mr. Cashmore added to this one. Now the
> question is: what is Mr. Cashmore? Here is the an-
> swer I shall give: Mr. Cashmore is (1) a noise, (2) a
> proper name, (3) a complex system of ideas, (4) a
> controlling perception, (5) an instrument of verbal
> organization, (6) a pretended mode of referring, and

(7) a source of verbal energy. He is not an object of
perception, and nothing whatever that is appropri-
ate to persons can be correctly said of him.*

Like much formalist criticism, this is both obviously right and obviously wrong. Of course
characters are assemblages of words, for literature is such an assemblage of words: this is like
informing us that a novel cannot *really* create an
imagined "world," because it is just a bound co-
dex of paper pages. Surely Mr. Cashmore, intro-
duced thus by James, has instantly become, in
practice, "an object of perception"—precisely
because we are looking at a description of him.
Gass claims, "Nothing whatever that is appro-
priate to persons can be correctly said of him,"
but that is exactly what James has just done: he
has said of him things that are usually said of a
real person. He has told us that Mr. Cashmore
looked bald and red, and that his "petulant
movements" seemed out of keeping with his
large jauntiness ("were not in the line of his
type"). At present, of course, in James's prelimi-
nary dabs, Mr. Cashmore has just been created,
and he hardly exists; Gass confuses the character's Edenic virginity with his later, fallen
essence. That's to say, Mr. Cashmore at this

Fiction and the Figures of Life (1970).

moment is like the frame of one of those buildings we look at from the street, and which so
often seem like stage sets. Of course "any number of other sentences about Mr. Cashmore"
could be added to the ones we have: that is
because so few sentences have so far been said
by James about him. The more paint that James
applies, the less provisional will the character
seem. "There are no descriptions in fiction, there
are only constructions," Gass argues in the same
book. But why one or the other? To my mind,
to deny character with such extremity is essentially to deny the novel.

67

But to repeat, what *is* a character? I am thick-
eted in qualifications: if I say that a character
seems connected to consciousness, to the use of
a mind, the many superb examples of characters
who seem to think very little, who are rarely
seen thinking, bristle up (Gatsby, Captain Ahab,
Becky Sharp, Widmerpool, Jean Brodie). If I re-
fine the thought by repeating that a character
at least has some essential connection to an interior life, to inwardness, is seen "from within,"
I am presented with the nicely opposing examples of those two adulterers, Anna Karenina and
Effi Briest, the first of whom does a lot of reflec-

tion, and is seen internally as well as externally, the second of whom, in Theodor Fontane's eponymous novel, is seen almost entirely from the outside, with little space set aside for represented reflection. No one could say that Anna is more vivid than Effi simply because we see Anna doing more thinking.

If I try to distinguish between major and minor characters—round and flat characters—and claim that these differ in terms of subtlety, depth, time allowed on the page, I must concede that many so-called flat characters seem more alive to me, and more interesting as human studies, however short-lived, than the round characters they are supposedly subservient to.

68

The novel is the great virtuoso of exceptionalism: it always wriggles out of the rules thrown around it. And the novelistic character is the very Houdini of that exceptionalism. There is no such thing as "a novelistic character." There are just thousands of different kinds of people, some round, some flat, some deep, some caricatures, some realistically evoked, some brushed in with the lightest of strokes. Some of them are solid enough that we can speculate about their motives: Why does Hurstwood steal the money?

Why does Isabel Archer return to Gilbert Osmond? What is Julien Sorel's true ambition?
Why does Kirilov want to commit suicide?
What does Mr. Biswas want? But there are scores
of fictional characters who are not fully or conventionally evoked who are also alive and vivid.
The solid, nineteenth-century fictional character
(I count Biswas in that company) who confronts
us with deep mysteries is not the "best" or ideal
or only way to create character (though it does
not deserve the enormous condescension of postmodernism). My own taste tends toward the
sketchier fictional personage, whose lacunae and
omissions tease us, provoke us to wade in their
deep shallows: Why does Onegin reject Tatiana
and then provoke a fight with Lenski? Pushkin
offers us almost no evidence on which to base
our answer. Is Svevo's Zeno mad? Is the narrator of Hamsun's *Hunger* mad? We have only their
unreliable narration of events.

69

Perhaps because I am not sure what a character
is, I find especially moving those postmodern
novels, like *Pnin*, or Muriel Spark's *The Prime of
Miss Jean Brodie*, or José Saramago's *The Year of
the Death of Ricardo Reis*, or Roberto Bolaño's *The
Savage Detectives*, or W. G. Sebald's *Austerlitz*, or

Ali Smith's *How to Be Both*, in which we are are confronted with characters who are at once real and unreal. In each of these novels, the author asks us to reflect on the fictionality of the heroes and heroines who give the novels their titles. And in a fine paradox, it is precisely such reflection that stirs in the reader a desire to make these fictional characters "real," to say, in effect, to the authors: "I know that they are only fictional— you keep on suggesting this. But I can only *know* them by treating them as real." That is how *Pnin* works, for instance. An unreliable narrator insists that Professor Pnin is "a character" in two senses of the word: a type (clownish, eccentric émigré) and a fictional character, the narrator's fantasy. Yet just because we resent the narrator's condescension toward his fond and foolish possession, we insist that behind the "type" there must be a real Pnin, who is worth "knowing" in all his fullness and complexity. And Nabokov's novel is constructed in such a way as to excite that desire in us for a real Professor Pnin, a "true fiction" with which to oppose the false fictions of the overbearing and sinister narrator.

70

José Saramago's great novel *The Year of the Death of Ricardo Reis* works a little differently, but to the same effect, and, like *Pnin*, becomes a moving investigation of what a real self is. Ricardo Reis, a doctor from Brazil, is an aloof, conservative aesthete who has decided to return to his native Portugal. It is the end of 1935, and the great poet Fernando Pessoa has just died. Reis is himself a poet and mourns Pessoa's departure. He is not sure what to do. He has saved some money, and for a while he lives in a hotel, where he has an affair with a chambermaid. He writes several beautiful lyrics, and is visited by the now-ghostly Pessoa, with whom he converses. Saramago describes these conversations in a frankly literal and direct manner. Reis wanders the streets of Lisbon, as 1935 curdles into 1936. He reads the newspapers, and is increasingly alarmed by the baying of Europe's dogs: in Spain civil war and the rise of Franco, in Germany Hitler, in Italy Mussolini, and in Portugal the fascist dictatorship of Salazar. He would like to retreat from this bad news. He reflects fondly on the story of the ninety-seven-year-old John D. Rockefeller, who has a specially doctored version of *The New York Times* delivered every day, altered to contain only good news. "The world's threats are universal, like the sun, but Ricardo Reis takes shelter under his own shadow."

But Ricardo Reis is not a "real" fictional character, whatever that means (like David Copperfield or Emma Bovary). He is one of the four pen names that the actual Pessoa—the poet who worked and lived in Lisbon and died in 1935—assumed, and in whose persona he wrote poetry. The special flicker of this book, the tint and the delicacy that make it seem hallucinatory, derive from the solidity with which Saramago invests a character who is fictional twice over: first Pessoa's, then Saramago's. This enables Saramago to tease us with something that we already know, namely that Ricardo Reis is fictional. Saramago makes something deep and moving of this because Ricardo also feels himself to be somewhat fictional, at best a shadowy spectator, a man on the margin of things. And when Ricardo reflects thus, we feel a strange tenderness for him, aware of something that *he does not know*, that he is not real.

71

Is there a way in which all of us are fictional characters, parented by life and written by ourselves? This is something like Saramago's question; but it is worth noting that he reaches his question by traveling in the opposite direction of those postmodern novelists who like to remind us of the metafictionality of all things. A certain kind of postmodern novelist (like John

Barth, say) is always lecturing us: "Remember, this character is just a character. I invented him." By starting with an invented character, however, Saramago is able to pass through the same skepticism, but in the opposite direction, toward reality, toward the deepest questions. Saramago asks, in effect: But what *is* "just a character"? And Saramago's uncertainty is more searching than William Gass's skepticism, for in life we anxiously question our existence rather than deny it.

In Saramago's novels, the self may cast only a shadow, like Ricardo Reis, but this shadow implies not the nonexistence of the self, but only its difficult visibility, its near invisibility, rather as the shadow cast by the sun warns us that we cannot look directly at it. Ricardo Reis is aloof, ghostly. He does not want to get pulled into real relationships, including the real relationships of politics. Europe is scrambling for war, but Ricardo luxuriously sits around wondering if he exists. He writes a poem that begins "We count for nothing, we are less than futile." Another poem begins: "Walk empty-handed, for wise is the man who contents himself with the spectacle of the world." Yet the novel suggests that perhaps there is something culpable about being content with the spectacle of the world when the world's spectacle is horrifying.

72

The question of this novel, and of much of Saramago's work, is not the trivial "metafictional"
game-playing of "Does Ricardo Reis exist?" It
is the much more poignant question, "Do we exist if we refuse to relate to anyone?"

73

What does it mean to "love" a fictional character, to feel that you know her? What kind of
knowledge is this? Miss Jean Brodie is one of the
best-loved novelistic characters in postwar British fiction, and one of the very few to be something of a household name. But if you dragged
a microphone down Princes Street in Edinburgh
and asked people what they "know" about Miss
Brodie, those who had read Muriel Spark's novel
would likely recite a number of her aphorisms:
"I am in my prime," "You are the crème de la
crème," "The Philistines are upon us, Mr. Lloyd,"
and so on. These are Jean Brodie's famous sayings. Miss Brodie, in other words, is not really
"known" at all. We know her just as her young
pupils knew her: as a collection of tags, a rhetorical performance, a teacher's show. At Marcia
Blaine School for Girls, each member of the Brodie set is "famous" for something: Mary Macgregor is famous for being stupid, and Rose is

famous for sex, and so on. Miss Brodie, it seems, is famous for her sayings. Around her very thinness as a character we tend to construct a thicker interpretative jacket.

Nearly all of Muriel Spark's novels are fiercely composed and devoutly starved. Her brilliantly reduced style, of "never apologize, never explain," seems a deliberate provocation: we feel compelled to turn the mere crescents of her characters into solid discs. But while some of her refusal to wax explanatory or sentimental may have been temperamental, it was also moral. Spark was intensely interested in how much we can know about anyone, and interested in how much a novelist, who most pretends to such knowledge, can know about her characters. By reducing Miss Brodie to no more than a collection of maxims, Spark forces *us* to become Brodie's pupils. In the course of the novel we never leave the school to go home with Miss Brodie. We never see her in private, offstage. Always, she is the performing teacher, keeping a public face. We surmise that there is something unfulfilled and even desperate about her, but the novelist refuses us access to her interior. Brodie talks a great deal about her prime, but we don't witness it, and the nasty suspicion falls that perhaps to talk so much about one's prime is by definition no longer to be in it.

Spark always exercises ruthless control over

her fictional characters, and here she flaunts it: she spikes her story with a series of "flash-forwards," in which we learn what happened to the characters after the main action of the plot (Miss Brodie will die of cancer, Mary Macgregor will die at the age of twenty-three in a fire, another pupil will join a convent, another will have an ordinary marriage, another will never again be quite as happy as when she first discovered algebra). These coldly prophetic passages strike some readers as cruel; they are such summary judgments. But they are moving, because they raise the idea that if Miss Brodie never really had a prime, then for some of the schoolgirls their primes occurred in their childhoods—during those days earnestly praised, at least by one's teachers, as the "happiest days of your life."

These flash-forwards do something else: they remind us that Muriel Spark has powers of ultimate control over her creations; and they remind us of . . . Miss Brodie. This tyrannical authority is precisely what Miss Brodie's most intelligent pupil, Sandy Stranger, hates, and finally exposes, in her teacher: that she is a fascist and a Scottish Calvinist, predestining the lives of her pupils, forcing them into artificial shapes. Is this what the novelist does, too? That is the question that interests Spark. The novelist adopts Godlike powers of omniscience, but what can she really know of her creations? Surely only God, the ultimate author of our lives, can know our coming and our going, and surely only God has the moral right to decide such things. Nabokov used to say that he pushed his characters around like serfs or chess pieces—he had no time for that metaphorical ignorance and impotence whereby authors like to say, "I don't know what happened, but my character just got away from me and did his own thing. I had nothing to do with it."* Nonsense, said Nabokov, if I want my character to cross the road, he crosses the road. I am his master. Nabokov's fiction, like Spark's, explores the implications of such potency: Timofey Pnin finally refuses to be pushed about by Nabokov's bullying narrator, who seems suspiciously like Nabokov himself. Pnin memorably says that he refuses to "work under" the narrator (who is coming to head the department where Professor Pnin teaches). This was one of Spark's abiding concerns, from her early novels like *The Comforters* and *Memento Mori* to her very last, *The Finishing School*. She used fiction to reflect on the responsibilities and limitations of fiction itself, and indeed on the difficulties and limitations of all fiction-making. (The Scottish

---

*As, by report, Pushkin spoke of Onegin and Tatiana: "Do you know my Tatiana has rejected Onegin? I never expected it of her."

novelist Ali Smith, a great admirer of Muriel Spark, continues this metafictional tradition, in a more exuberant and playful vein.)

74

This fictional self-consciousness, and her devotion to spare forms, made Spark resemble at times a *nouveau romancier* like Alain Robbe-Grillet or the British avant-gardist B. S. Johnson, who once published a novel, *The Unfortunates*, made of looseleaf pages in a box, to be arranged as the reader saw fit. Johnson's slightly more conventional novel, *Christie Malry's Own Double-Entry*, is very funny, and studded with amusing metafictional self-consciousness. Christie's mother says things like: "My son: I have for the purposes of this novel been your mother for the past eighteen years and five months to the day . . ." At his mother's funeral, "Christie was the only mourner, economy as to relatives (as to so many other things) being one of the virtues of this novel." Like Nabokov and Spark, B. S. Johnson saw the comparison between God the omniscient author and the omnipotent novelist, who can do anything he likes with his "chess pieces." At one point, Christie's mother explains how Adam and Eve first ate from the tree. Of course, she says, the whole thing is absurd, because God could

have stopped it any time He liked, being omniscient. "But no: God has been making it all up as
He goes along, like certain kinds of novelist . . ."

But the difference between Johnson and Spark
is instructive, too. Johnson plays with these
questions but does not finally *inhabit* them as
Spark or Nabokov or Saramago does. In the end
there is nothing like the pressure of inquiry you
feel in those writers. Johnson is content to ask,
again and again—and very entertainingly—the
metafictional question "Does Christie exist?" but
not the metaphysical question "How does Christie exist?"—which is really the question "How
do *we* exist?" The reason for the atmosphere of
postmodern lightness in this novel is that Johnson is not able to be gravely skeptical, because
he is not able to be gravely affirmative (the opposite of Saramago, as we saw, who wrings skepticism out of affirmation). Jean Brodie, though
we see her in only a handful of scenes that are
shuffled like a pack of cards, *exists* for Spark, has
metaphysical presence, and does for us, too. That
is why the questions "Who was Jean Brodie?
Who really knew her?" have power and affect.
But Christie Malry does not really exist for Johnson. He is denied before he is believed in.*

---

*Philip Roth's *The Counterlife* is an example of another novel that takes
what it needs from metafictional game-playing to make a grave and fun-

75

To argue that we can know Jean Brodie just as
deeply as we can know Dorothea Brooke, to
argue that lacunae are as deep as solidities, that
absence in characterization can be a form of
knowing as profound as presence, that Spark's
and Saramago's and Nabokov's characters can
move us as much as James's and Eliot's, is to concede little to William Gass's skepticism. Not
all of these characters have the same amount of
realized "depth," but all of them are objects of
perception, to use Gass's words, all of them are
more than mere bundles of words (though of
course they *are* bundles of words), and things
that can be correctly said of persons can also be
said of them. They are all "real" (they have a
reality) but in different ways. That reality level
differs from author to author, and our hunger for
the particular depth or reality level of a character is tutored by each writer, and adapts to the

damental metaphysical argument about the different ways of living,
and narrating, a life. Gabriel Josipovici discusses Beckett in this spirit in
his book *On Trust* (2000). He points out that Foucault liked to quote
from *The Unnamable*, as evidence of the death of the author: "No matter
who is speaking, someone says, no matter who is speaking," wrote Beckett. Josipovici comments that Foucault forgets that "it is not Beckett
saying this but one of his characters, and that the point about that character is that he is desperately seeking to discover *who* speaks, to recover
himself as more than a string of words, to wrest an 'I' from 'someone
says.'"

internal conventions of each book. This is how we can read W. G. Sebald one day, and Woolf the next, and Philip Roth the next, and not demand that each resemble the other. It would be an obvious category mistake to accuse Sebald of not offering us "deep" or "rounded" characters, or to accuse Woolf of not offering us plenty of juicy, robust minor characters in the way of Dickens. I think that novels tend to fail not when the characters are not vivid or deep enough, but when the novel in question has failed to teach us how to adapt to its conventions, has failed to manage a specific hunger for its own characters, its own reality level. In such cases, our appetite is quickly disappointed, and surges wildly in excess of what we are provided, and we tend to blame the author for not giving us enough—the characters, we complain, are not alive or round or free enough. Yet we would not dream of accusing Sebald or Woolf or Roth— none of whom is especially interested in creating character in the solid, old-fashioned nineteenth-century sense—of letting us down in this way, because they have so finely tutored us in their own conventions, their own expansive limitations, to be satisfied with just what they give us.

76

Even the characters we think of as "solidly realized" in the conventional realist sense are less
solid the longer we look at them. I think there
is a basic distinction to be made between novelists like Tolstoy or Trollope or Balzac or Dickens, or dramatists like Shakespeare, who are
rich in "negative capability," who seem unself-
consciously to create galleries of various people
who are nothing like them, and those writers
either less interested in, or perhaps less naturally
gifted at this faculty, but who nevertheless have
a great deal of interest in the self—James, Flaubert, Lawrence, Woolf perhaps, Musil, Bellow,
Michel Houellebecq, Philip Roth, Lydia Davis.
Bellow's vibrating individuals are Dickensianly
vivid, and Bellow himself was aesthetically and
philosophically interested in the individual, but
no one would call him a great creator of fictional
individuals. We don't go around saying to ourselves, "What would Augie March or Charlie Ci-
trine do?"* Iris Murdoch is the most poignant
member of this second category, precisely
because she spent her life trying to get into the
first. In her literary and philosophical criticism,
she again and again stresses that the creation of

---

*Except for the hero and narrator of Frederick Exley's one good novel,
A Fan's Notes, who explicitly invokes the example of Augie.

free and independent characters is the mark of
the great novelist; yet her own characters never
have this freedom. She knew it, too: "How soon
one discovers that, however much one is in the
ordinary sense 'interested in other people,' this
interest has left one far short of possessing the
knowledge required to create a character who is
not oneself. It is impossible, it seems to me, not
to see one's failure here as a sort of spiritual
failure."*

77

But Murdoch is too unforgiving of herself. There
are scores of novelists whose characters are basically like each other, or rather like the novelist
who created them, and yet whose creations
stream with a vitality that it would be hard not
to call free. Does *The Rainbow* possess any characters who don't sound like each other, and ultimately like D. H. Lawrence? Tom Brangwen,
Will, Anna, Ursula, even Lydia—they are all
variations on a Lawrencian theme, and despite
differences in articulacy and education, their
inner lives vibrate very similarly. When they
speak, which is rarely, they sound the same.

---

*"The Sublime and the Beautiful Revisited," in *Existentialists and Mys-
tics: Writings on Philosophy and Literature* (1997).

Nevertheless, they do possess blazing inner lives, and always one feels how important this inquiry into the state of the soul is for the novelist himself. In some sense, the scenes—the battles of husband and wife, of two opposed and proximate egos—are more individuated than the characters themselves: Will and Anna stacking sheaves of corn in the harvest moonlight; the chapter called "Anna Victrix," which describes the first, swooning months of the marriage, as Will and Anna discover the sublimity of their sexual union and realize that the world is insignificant to the passion they share; pregnant Anna dancing naked in her bedroom, as David once danced before the Lord, while Will looks on enviously; the chapter devoted to the visit to Lincoln Cathedral; the great flood, which kills Tom Brangwen; Ursula and Skrebensky, kissing under the moon; Ursula at the oppressive school in Ilkeston; Skrebensky and Ursula running away to London and Paris—in a London hotel room she watches him bathing: "He was slender, and, to her, perfect, a clean, straight-cut youth, without a grain of superfluous body."

In the same way, it often seems that James's characters are not especially convincing as independently vivid authorial creations. But what makes them vivid is the force of James's interest in them, his manner of pressing into their clay with his examining fingers: they are sites of human energy; they vibrate with James's anxious concern for them. Take *The Portrait of a Lady*. It is very hard to say what Isabel Archer is *like*, exactly, and she seems to lack the definition, the depth if you like, of a heroine like Dorothea Brooke, in *Middlemarch*.

I think this was deliberate on James's part. His novel begins with extraordinary stiffness and self-consciousness: three men, engaged in frivolous badinage, are sitting having tea, waiting for the arrival of the host's niece. They talk about this lady. Isn't she due soon? Will she be pretty? Perhaps one of the men will marry her? And then at the very start of the second chapter, she obligingly arrives. Were James being "workshopped" in a creative writing course, he would be censured for this speedy awkwardness; he should surely put a chapter of naturalistic filler between the men at tea and the arrival, make it look a bit less novelistic and convenient. But James's point is that these men—and by extension we the readers—are waiting for the arrival of a *heroine*; and, sure enough, here is the author stepping up to provide her. James then proceeds, over the next forty or so pages, to hand us an enormous plate of commentary about Isabel, much of it contradictory. It is presented to us by the author in full exegetical mode. Isabel is brilliant, but perhaps only by the standards of provincial Albany; Isabel wants freedom, but really she is afraid of it; Isabel wants to suffer, but really she doesn't believe in suffering; she is egotistical, but she likes nothing better than to humble herself; and so on. It is essentially a mess of propositions, and there is very little attempt to present Isabel dramatically. It is an essay, an essay on a character. And it is mostly James telling and not showing.

78

James is really suggesting that he has not yet formed his character, that she is still relatively shapeless, an American emptiness, and that the *novel* will form her, for good and ill, that Europe will fill in her shape, and that just as these three waiting, watching men will also form her, so will we, as readers. They and we are a kind of Greek chorus, hanging on her every move. Two of the men, Lord Warburton and Ralph Touchett, will devote their lives to watching her. And what, James asks, will be the plot that poor Isabel will have written for herself? How much will she herself write it, and how much will be written for her by others? And in the end, will we really know what Isabel was like, or will we have merely painted a portrait of a lady?

So the vitality of literary character has less to do with dramatic action, novelistic coherence, and even plain plausibility—let alone likeability—than with a larger philosophical or metaphysical sense, our awareness that a character's actions are deeply *important*, that something profound is at stake, with the author brooding over the face of that character like God over the face of the waters. That is how readers retain in their minds a sense of the character "Isabel Archer," even if they cannot tell you what she is exactly like. We remember her in the way we remember an obscurely significant day: something important has been enacted here.

79

In *Aspects of the Novel*, Forster used the now-famous term "flat" to describe the kind of character who is awarded a single, essential attribute, which is repeated without change as the person appears and reappears in a novel. Often, such characters have a catchphrase or tagline or keyword, as Mrs. Micawber, in *David Copperfield*, likes to repeat, "I never will desert Mr. Micawber." She says she will not, and she does not. Forster is genially snobbish about flat characters, and wants to demote them, reserving the highest category for rounder, or fuller, characters. Flat

characters cannot be tragic, he asserts; they need
to be comic. Round characters "surprise" us
each time they reappear; they are not flimsily
theatrical; they combine well with other characters in conversation, "and draw one another
out without seeming to do so." Flat ones can't
surprise us, and are generally monochromati-
cally histrionic. Forster mentions a popular
novel by a contemporary novelist whose main
character, a flat one, is a farmer who is always
saying, "I'll plough up that bit of gorse." But,
says Forster, we are so bored by the farmer's consistency that we do not care whether he does or
doesn't. Mrs. Micawber, he suggests, has a saving
comic lightness, which allows her to be similarly
consistent but not similarly dull.

But is this right? Of course, we know a caricature when we see one, and caricature is generally uninteresting. (Though sometimes it might
just be a novelist's way of sticking to the
point . . .) But if by flatness we mean a character, often but not always a minor one, often but
not always comic, who serves to illuminate an
essential human truth or characteristic, then
many of the most interesting characters are flat.
I would be quite happy to abolish the very idea
of "roundness" in characterization, because it
tyrannizes us—readers, novelists, critics—with
an impossible ideal. "Roundness" is impossible

in fiction, because fictional characters, while very
alive in their way, are not the same as real people
(though, of course, there are many real people,
in real life, who are quite flat and don't seem
very round—which I will come to). It is subtlety
that matters—subtlety of analysis, of inquiry, of
concern, of felt pressure—and for subtlety a very
small point of entry will do. Forster's division
grandly privileges novels over short stories, since
characters in stories rarely have the space to become "round." But I learn more about the consciousness of the soldier in Chekhov's "The Kiss"
than I do about the consciousness of Becky Sharp
in *Vanity Fair*, because Chekhov's inquiry into
how his soldier's mind works is more acute than
Thackeray's serial vividness.*

---

*Spatial metaphors, of depth, shallowness, roundness, flatness, are inad-
equate. A better division—though not perfect, either—is between
transparencies (relatively simple characters) and opacities (relative de-
grees of mysteriousness). Many of the most absorbing accounts of motive, from Hamlet to Stavrogin to the subjects of W. G. Sebald's *The
Emigrants*, are studies in mystery. Stephen Greenblatt argues in *Will in
the World: How Shakespeare Became Shakespeare* (2004) that in his trage-
dies, Shakespeare systematically reduced the amount of "causal explanation a tragic plot needed to function effectively and the amount of
explicit psychological rationale a character needed to be compelling.
Shakespeare found that he could immeasurably deepen the effect of his
plays, that he could provoke in the audience and in himself a peculiarly
passionate intensity of response, if he took out a key explanatory element, thereby occluding the rationale, motivation, or ethical principle
that accounted for the action that was to unfold. The principle was not the
making of a riddle to be solved, but the creation of a strategic opacity."

In the second place, many of the most vivid characters in fiction are monomaniacs. There is Hardy's Michael Henchard, in *The Mayor of Casterbridge*, who burns with his one secret, or Gould in *Nostromo*, who can think only of his mine. Casaubon, too, fixated on his infinite book. Aren't such people essentially flat? They may surprise us at first, but they soon stop surprising us, as their central need occupies them. Yet they are no less vivid, interesting, or true as creations, for being flat. They are certainly not cartoons, which is implicit in Forster's discussion. (They are not cartoons because their monomania is not inherently cartoonish but inherently interesting—*consistently surprising*, one might say.)

Forster struggles to explain how we feel that most of Dickens's characters are flat and yet at the same time that these cameos obscurely move us—he claims that Dickens's own vitality makes

---

Why does Lear test his daughters? Why can't Hamlet effectively avenge the death of his father? Why does Iago ruin Othello's life? The source texts that Shakespeare read all provided transparent answers (Iago was in love with Desdemona, Hamlet should kill Claudius, Lear was unhappy with Cordelia's impending marriage). But Shakespeare was not interested in such transparency. Greenblatt's argument also touches on section 88, where I show how the novel threw off the essential juvenility of plot in favor of "unconsummated" stories, and section 111, where I discuss the novel's possible contribution to Bernard Williams's desire for complexity in moral philosophy.

them "vibrate" a bit on the page. But this vibrating flatness is true not only of Dickens, but also of Proust, who also likes to tag many of his characters with favorite sayings and catchphrases, of Tolstoy to some extent, of Hardy's minor characters, of Mann's minor characters (he, like Proust and Tolstoy, uses a method of mnemonic leitmotif—a repeated attribute or characteristic—to secure the vitality of his characters), and supremely of Jane Austen.

80

Forster mysteriously claims Austen for the round character camp, but in doing so he just shows that he needs to expand his definition of flatness. For what is striking about Austen is precisely that only her heroines are really capable of development and surprise: they are the only characters who possess consciousness, the only characters who are seen thinking in any depth, and they are heroic, in part, *because* they possess the secret of consciousness. The minor characters around them, by contrast, are pretty obviously flat. They are seen externally, they reveal themselves only in speech, and little is demanded of them: Mr. Collins, Miss Bates, Mr. Woodhouse, and so on. The minor characters belong to a certain stage of theatrical satire; the heroines belong to the newly emergent, newly complex form of the novel.

Take Shakespeare's *Henry V* as an example. If you asked most people to separate King Harry and the Welsh captain Fluellen into Forsterian camps, they would award Harry roundness and Fluellen flatness. The king is a large part, Fluellen a minor one. Harry talks and reflects a lot, he soliloquizes, he is noble, canny, magniloquent, and surprising: he goes among his soldiers in disguise, to talk freely with them. He complains of the burden of kingship. Fluellen, by contrast, is a comic Welshman, a pedant of the kind Fielding or Cervantes would nimbly satirize, always banging on about military history, and Alexander the Great, and leeks, and Monmouth. Harry rarely makes us laugh, Fluellen always does. Harry is round, Fluellen flat. Which actor, at audition, would choose Fluellen over the part of the king? ("I'm sorry sir, Mr. Branagh has already reserved that part for himself.")

But the categories could easily go the other way. The King Harry of this play, unlike the Harry of the two *Henry IV* plays, is merely kingly, in rather a dull fashion. He is very eloquent, but it seems like Shakespeare's eloquence, not his own (it's formal, patriotic, august). His complaints about the burdens of kingship are a bit formulaic and self-pitying, and tell us little about his actual self (except, in a generic way, that he is self-pitying). He is an utterly public figure. Fluellen, by contrast, is a little terrier of vividness. His speech, despite the "Welshisms" that Shakespeare puts in—"look you," and so on—is idiosyncratically his own. He is a pedant, but an interesting one. In Fielding, a pedantic doctor or lawyer speaks like a pedantic doctor or lawyer: his pedantry is professionally bound up with his occupation. But Fluellen's pedantry has a limitless and slightly desperate quality about it: Why does he know so much about the classics, about Alexander the Great and Philip of Macedon? Why has he appointed himself the army's military historian? He surprises us, too: at first we think his windiness will substitute for valor on the field, as Falstaff's did, because we think we recognize a type—the man who speaks about military action rather than performing it. But he turns out to possess a touching valor and loyalty; and his rectitude—another inversion of type—is not merely hypocritical. (That is, he does not *just* talk about rectitude, even though he does indeed talk a lot about it.) And there is something piquant about a man who is at once an omnivorous roamer of the world's knowledge and literatures, and at the same time a little Welsh provincial. His monologue on how Monmouth resembles the classical city of Macedon is both funny and moving:

> I tell you, captain, if you look in the maps of the worlds I warrant you shall find, in the comparisons between Macedon and Monmouth, that the situations, look you, is both alike. There is a river in Macedon, and there is also moreover a river at Monmouth.

I still meet people like Fluellen; and when a garrulous guy on a train starts talking up his hometown, and says something like "we've got one of those"—shopping mall, opera house, violent bar—"in my town, too, you know," you are apt to feel, as toward Fluellen, both mirth and an obscure kind of sympathy, since this kind of importuning provincialism is always paradoxical: the provincial simultaneously wants and does not want to communicate with you, simultaneously wants to remain a provincial and abolish his provincialism by linking himself with you. Almost four hundred years later, in a story called "The Wheelbarrow," V. S. Pritchett revisits Fluellen. A Welsh taxi driver, Evans, is helping a lady clear out a house. He finds an old volume of verse in a box, and suddenly bursts out, scornfully: "Everyone knows that the Welsh are the founders of all the poetry in Europe."

81

In fact, the ubiquitous flat character of the English novel, from Mr. Collins to Charles Ryder's father, tells us something deep about the dialectic of British reticence and sociability, and something, too, about British theatricality. It is hardly surprising that the self should be so often theatrical in English fiction, when its great progenitor is Shakespeare. But of course many of Shakespeare's characters are not just theatrical; they are self-theatricalzing. They carry within them fantastic, often illusory, notions of their own prowess and reputation. This is true of Lear, of Antony, of Cleopatra, of Richard II, of Falstaff, of Othello (who, as he is dying, is still instructing his audience to make a record of his demise: "Set you down this, / And say besides that in Aleppo once, / . . . I took by th' throat the circumcised dog / And smote him thus"). And it is true, too, of the minor characters like Launce and Bottom and Mistress Quickly, who so easily flame up into histrionic comic irrelevance.

From Shakespeare descends a self-theatricalizing, somewhat solipsistic, flamboyant, but also perhaps essentially shy type who can be found in Fielding, Austen, Dickens, Hardy, Thackeray, Meredith, Wells, Henry

Green, Evelyn Waugh, V. S. Pritchett, Muriel
Spark, Angus Wilson, Martin Amis, Zadie
Smith, and on into the superb pantomimic em-
barrassments of Monty Python and Ricky Ger-
vais's David Brent. He is typified by Mr. Omer,
in *David Copperfield*, the tailor whom David visits to get his funeral suit. (David is en route to
his mother's funeral.) Mr. Omer is an English so-
liloquist, and prattles on without embarrassment as he blunders his way all over David's
grief: "showing me a roll of cloth which he said
was extra super, and too good mourning for anything short of parents," and saying, "'But fashions are like human beings. They come in,
nobody knows when, why, or how; and they go
out, nobody knows when, why, or how. Everything is like life, in my opinion, if you look at it
in that point of view.'"

Something true is revealed here about the self
and its irrepressibility or irresponsibility—the
little riot of freedom in otherwise orderly souls,
the self's chink of freedom, its gratuity or surplus, its tip to itself. Mr. Omer is determined to
be himself, even if that means likening fashions
in clothes to patterns of morbidity. Yet no one
would call Mr. Omer a "round" character. He
exists for a bare minute. But contra Forster,
the flat character like Mr. Omer is indeed capable

of "surprising us"—the point is, *he only needs to surprise us once*, and can then disappear off the stage.

Mrs. Micawber's catchphrase, "I never will desert Mr. Micawber," tells us something true about how she keeps up appearances, how she maintains a theatrical public fiction, and so it tells us something true about *her*; but the farmer who says, "I'll plough up that bit of gorse" is not maintaining any similarly interesting fiction about himself—he is just being stoical or habitual—and so we know nothing about his true self behind the catchphrase. He is simply stating his agronomic intentions. That is why he is boring; "consistency" has nothing to do with it. And we all know people in real life who, like Mrs. Micawber, do indeed use a series of jingles and tags and repetitive gestures to maintain a certain kind of performance.

82

One reason that Cervantes needs to have Don Quixote accompanied by Sancho Panza on his travels is that the knight must have someone to talk to. When Don Quixote sends Sancho off to search for Dulcinea, and is alone for the first extended period in the novel, he does not *think*, as we would now understand the term. He speaks out aloud, he soliloquizes.

The novel begins in the theater, and novelistic characterization begins when the soliloquy goes inward. The soliloquy, in turn, has its origins in prayer, as we can see from Greek tragedy, or from Book 5 of *The Odyssey*, or from the Psalms, or from David's songs to the Lord in 1 and 2 Samuel. Shakespeare's heroes and heroines still use soliloquy to invoke the gods, if not quite to pray to them: "Come you spirits / That tend on mortal thoughts, unsex me here," "Blow, winds, and crack your cheeks!" and so on. The actor comes to the front of the stage and speaks his mind to an audience, who is both God above and we spectators in the seats. Nineteenth-century novelists like Charlotte Brontë and

Thomas Hardy continued to describe their characters as "soliloquizing" when speaking to themselves.

The novel has changed the art of characterization partly by changing *who a character is being seen by.* Consider three men, each permanently affected by a chance occurrence: King David in the Old Testament; Macbeth; and Raskolnikov in *Crime and Punishment.* David, strolling on his roof, sees Bathsheba, naked, bathing herself, and is instantly struck with lust. His decision to take her as his lover and wife, and to kill her inconvenient husband, sets in train a series of events that will lead to his downfall and his punishment by God. Macbeth is instantly contaminated by the suggestion of the three witches that he kill the king and take his mantle. He, too, is punished—if not explicitly by God, then by "evenhanded justice," and by "pity, like a naked newborn babe." And Raskolnikov, in a story clearly influenced by Shakespeare's play, is similarly polluted by an idea—that by killing a miserable pawnbroker, he can vaunt himself over ordinary morality like a Napoleon. He, too, must "accept his punishment," as Dostoevsky puts it, and be corrected by God.

83

Despite the many revelations and subtleties of the Old Testament narrative—David's political canniness, his sorrow at the way Saul treats him, his lust for Bathsheba, his grief at the death of his son, Absalom—David remains a public character. In the modern sense, he has no privacy. He hardly ever speaks his inner thoughts to himself; he speaks to God, and his soliloquies are prayers. He is external to us because in some way he *does not exist for us*, but for the Lord. He is seen by the Lord, is transparent to the Lord, but remains opaque to us. This opacity allows for a lovely margin of surprise, to use E. M. Forster's word. For instance, David is cursed by God, who tells him, through the offices of Nathan the prophet, that the house of David will be punished, beginning with his son. And indeed, David's son dies soon after birth. David's response is curious. While the child is ill, he fasts and weeps, but as soon as the child has died, he washes, changes his clothes, worships God, and asks his servants to put out food. When they ask him why he has acted thus, he replies: "While the child was still alive I fasted and wept, for I thought, 'Who knows, the LORD may favor me and the child will live.' And now that he is dead, why should I fast? Can I bring him back again? I am going to him and he will not come back to me" (2 Samuel 12:22–23). Robert Alter, whose modern English translation this is, comments: "David here acts in a way that neither his courtiers nor the audience of the story could have anticipated."

David's calm, massive resignation ("I am going to him and he will not come back to me") is beautiful, as well as surprising. David is "light in spirit." Despite God's curse, despite the loss of this son, and of Absalom, David dies peacefully in his bed, telling his son Solomon, "I go the way of all the earth."

David is opaque to us, one feels, precisely because he is transparent to God, who is his real audience. What matters to the Bible writer is not the state of David's mind, but the whole story, the entirety of the arc of David's life. And this story, this arc, is both human and not quite human—not quite, because causation is divine as well as human. David's life is determined partly by what he does, but the rest of his life is then overdetermined, one might say, by God's punishment of him. In a sense, the storyteller is God, who is writing fate's script. David does not have a mind, as we understand modern subjectivity. He has no past, to speak of, and no memory, for it is God's memory that counts, which never forgets. And when he sees Bathsheba, what happens to him is not an idea, or at least not in the way that Jesus, that cheerless psychologist, meant when he said that for a man to look lustfully upon a woman is already to commit adultery. Jesus here announces that mental states are as important as actions. But for the writer of the David story, the mental state is precisely what is occluded; action is all: "and he saw from the roof a woman bathing, and the woman was very beautiful. And David sent and inquired after the woman, and the one he sent said, 'Why, this is Bathsheba daughter of Eliam, wife of Uriah the Hittite.' And David sent messengers and fetched her and she came to him and he lay with her, she having just cleansed herself of her impurity, and she returned to her house. And the woman became pregnant . . ." David sees, and acts. As far as the narrative is concerned, he does not think.

84

Macbeth is not being seen by God so much as he is being seen by us, the audience. His prayers, you might say, are soliloquies, and get very close to mental thought, as he agonizes before us over the dilemma he finds himself in. One reason for the play's power has to do with its domestic intimacy, whereby we feel we are eavesdropping on the horrid privacy of the Macbeths' marriage, not to mention the guilt-tainted outpourings of their monologues. At certain moments, the play seems to want to pull away and develop itself into a new form, the form of the novel. At the banquet, for instance, in Act 3, Scene 4, when Macbeth sees Banquo's ghost, Lady Macbeth twice leans over to him, and attempts to strengthen his resolve. We have to imagine the characters almost whispering to each other in the presence of their guests. "What, quite unmanned in folly?" says Lady Macbeth. "If I stand here, I saw him," replies Macbeth. "Fie, for shame!" is the fierce spousal response. This is always awkward when acted onstage, because the attendant lords must murmur in the background—in an unconvincing, stagy way—as if they cannot hear what is being said. The privacy of the marital conversation is what poses a theatrical difficulty: Where, onstage, can it realistically happen? I think Shakespeare is essentially being a novelist at such moments. On the page, of course, such moments have as much space to exist as the novelist feels like awarding; it is a simple matter of the adjustment of point of view ("Lady Macbeth turned quickly to her blanched lord, gripped his hand with sharp nails, and hissed at him, 'What, quite unmanned in folly?'").

David's story is almost entirely public; Macbeth's is one of publicized privacy. And this private man differs from David in being the possessor of a memory. It is the memory—"the warder of the brain"—that will not leave Macbeth alone. "My dull brain was wrought / With things forgotten," says Macbeth, pathetically, but the play in fact bodies forth De Quincey's terrifying, pre-Freudian admonition in his *Confessions of an English Opium-Eater*: "There is no such thing as forgetting." So the real curse on the Macbeths is not theological, despite the machinery of the witches, and the ghosts; the real curse is mental, "the written troubles of the brain." Now a character's thought can be *retrospective*, can move back and forth over the present and the past, to take in a whole life:

> I have lived long enough. My way of life
> Is fall'n into the sere, the yellow leaf,
> And that which should accompany old age,
> As honour, love, obedience, troops of friends,
> I must not look to have . . .

85

If Macbeth's story is one of publicized privacy, Raskolnikov's story is one of scrutinized privacy. God still exists, but he is not watching Raskolnikov—at least, not until the end of the novel when Raskolnikov accepts Christ. Until that moment, Raskolnikov is being watched by us, the readers. The crucial difference between this and the theater is that we are invisible. In David's story the audience is in some important way irrelevant; in Macbeth's the audience is visible and silent, and soliloquy does indeed have the feeling not only of an address to an audience but of a conversation with an interlocutor—us—who will not respond, a blocked dialogue. In Raskolnikov's story the audience—the reader—is invisible but all-seeing; so the reader has replaced David's God and Macbeth's audience.

86

What are the implications of this enormous shift? The obvious one is that soliloquy does not have to be voiced, and can get closer to being true mental speech. The hero is released from the tyranny of necessary eloquence; he is an ordinary man. (This is just what Raskolnikov cannot bear.) Inner soliloquy can indulge in repetition, ellipsis, hysteria, vagueness—mental stutter. If Shakespeare's characters often seem to be overhearing themselves when they soliloquize,* *we* are now overhearing Raskolnikov.

---

*This is Harold Bloom's formulation, in *The Western Canon* (1994) and elsewhere, borrowed from Hegel.

There is no facet of his soul not tilted toward us. Something else worth noticing is that while David has no mind, to speak of, and Macbeth's mind is punished, Raskolnikov's mind is the author of its own woe; the idea of murdering the woman was his free invention.

Under the new dispensation of the invisible audience, the novel becomes the great analyst of unconscious motive, since the character is released from having to voice his motives: the reader becomes the hermeneut, looking between the lines for the *actual* motive. On the other hand, the absence of a visible audience seems to make the ordinary man *seek* an audience, in ways that would have seemed grotesque to lordly figures like the Macbeths. Many of the characters in *Crime and Punishment* seem compelled to act out horrid pantomimes and melodramas, in which they stage a version of themselves, for effect. David and Macbeth were men of action— you might say they were naturally dramatic (they knew who their audiences were); Raskolnikov is unnaturally theatrical, or better still, histrionic: he seeks attention, and he is desperately unstable and inauthentic, hiding at one moment, confessing at another, proud in one scene, self-abasing in the next. In the novel, we can see the self better than any literary form has yet allowed; but it is not going too far to say that the self is driven mad by being so invisibly scrutinized.

87

The novel has shown a stunning technical progression in its ability to render plot, and in making us attend to psychological motivation. In his essay "The End of the Novel," Osip Mandelstam claimed that "the novel was perfected and strengthened over an extremely long period of time as the art form to interest the reader in the fate of the individual," singling out two technical refinements:

1. The transformation of biography (the saint's life, the moralizing Theophrastan sketch, and so on) into a meaningful narrative or plot.
2. "Psychological motivation."

88

Adam Smith, in his *Lectures on Rhetoric and Belles Lettres*, complains of the relatively young form of the novel that "as newness is the only merit in a Novel and curiosity the only motive which induces us to read them, the writers are necessitated to make use of this method [i.e., suspense] to keep it up." This is an early, mid-eighteenth-

century attack on the mindlessness of suspense—
the kind of complaint nowadays made routinely
about thrillers and pulp fiction.

But the novel soon showed itself willing to
surrender the essential juvenility of suspense, in
favor of what Viktor Shklovsky calls "unconsummated" stories with "false endings" (he was
referring to Flaubert and Chekhov, respectively).*
To return to the case of Iris Murdoch, who so
wanted to create free characters and so often
failed, her failure is not one of psychological attention or metaphysical shallowness—quite the
opposite—but a Fielding-like devotion to exces-
sive plot-making. Her improbable, melodra-
matic, feeble stories, still highly indebted to
eighteenth- and nineteenth-century theatrics, are
not adult enough to take the strain of her complex moral analysis.†

*Theory of Prose, translated by Benjamin Sher, 1990.
†To my mind, this is also a weakness with a certain kind of postmodern
novel—say Thomas Pynchon's Against the Day—still in love with the
rapid, farcelike, overlit simplicities of Fielding. There is nothing more
eighteenth-century than Pynchon's love of picaresque plot accumulation;
his mockery of pedantry, which is at the same time a love of pedantry;
his habit of making his flat characters dance for a moment on stage and
then whisking them away; his vaudevillian fondness for silly names,
japes, mishaps, disguises, silly errors, and so on. There are pleasures to
be had from these amiable, peopled canvases, and there are passages of
great beauty, but, as in farce, the cost to final seriousness is considerable:
everyone is ultimately protected from real menace because no one really
exists. The massive turbines of the incessant story-making produce so

89

As Mandelstam suggested, the novel probably
has its origins in a secular response to the religious lives and biographies of saints and holy
men, and in the tradition inaugurated by the
Greek writer Theophrastus, who offered a series
of sketches of types—the miser, the hypocrite,
the fond and foolish lover, and so on. (*Don Quixote* belongs to the modern novel in part because
Cervantes is so determined to discredit the
"holy," chivalric tales of Arthur and Amadis of
Gaul.) Since these were discrete portraits, you
could not contrast one with the other.

The Theophrastan and religious tendency re-
mained strong in the novel throughout the eighteenth and nineteenth centuries, and is still
visible in cinema and in various kinds of pulp
fiction: villains are villains, heroes are heroes,
and the good and the bad are clearly separated
and delineated—think of Fielding, Goldsmith,
Scott, Dickens, Waugh. Character is essentially
stable, has fixed attributes, in such writers.

But at the same time, another kind of novel
was developing, in which good and bad wars

---

much noise that no one can be heard. The Nazi Captain Blicero in *Grav-
ity's Rainbow*, or the ruthless financier Scarsdale Vibe in *Against the Day*,
are not truly frightening figures, because they are not true figures. But
Gilbert Osmond, Herr Naphta, Peter Verkhovensky, and Conrad's anar-
chist professor are very frightening indeed.

within a single character, and the self refuses to
stay still. What the novel powerfully began to
do was to explore characterological relativity.
This tradition in turn would influence the English and American novel in the early decades
of the twentieth century, particularly as Dostoevsky began to be translated into English (Lawrence, Conrad, Ford, and Woolf were the chief
beneficiaries). And all this can be traced pretty
much to one extraordinary novel, *Rameau's
Nephew*, written by Denis Diderot in the 1760s,
though not published until 1784. In this furious dialogue (it is laid out on the page like a
play) an obscure nephew of the famous composer
Jean-Philippe Rameau engages in a fictional encounter with an interlocutor named "Diderot."
Rameau's nephew seems, at first, a recognizable
enough French type—a sophisticated cynic, a
man who sees through society, a Juvenal of the
Luxembourg Gardens. But Diderot's brilliant
addition is to complicate this figure by making
him resentfully dependent on his famous uncle,
the composer. Rameau's nephew plays party
tricks like mimicking his uncle's music, which
he says he finds boring, by sitting at a fake piano, playing fake music, all the while grimac-
ing and sweating and crooning. He is very
unstable; he is described by Diderot as someone
who changes from month to month. There is a

hollowness, too, because he wants to be famous: "I would like to be somebody else, at the risk of being a man of genius, a great man . . . Yes, yes, I am mediocre and angry." He says that he has never listened to his uncle's music without ruefully thinking, "That's what you will never do." He dilates on his envy: "I who have composed keyboard pieces which nobody plays, but which may well be the only ones to go down to future generations who will." He admires the criminal's daring alienation from society, as Raskolnikov will do.

Where his interlocutor—the Diderot figure—sees reason and order in society, Rameau sees only hypocrisy. The Diderot figure says that he constantly reads "La Bruyère, Molière, and Theophrastus"—the didactic creators of stable, moralizing, satiric characterization. He says that such writers teach knowledge of one's duties, love of virtue, hatred of vice, which is exactly what we would expect him pompously to say. Rameau's nephew replies that all he has learned from these writers is the value of fraudulence and hypocrisy: "When I read *Tartuffe* I tell myself: 'be a hypocrite, by all means, but don't talk like one. Keep the vices that come in useful to you, but don't have either the tone or the appearance, which would expose you to ridicule.'" (Through this conversation, Diderot makes his comment on the kind of simpler characterization that his own book has outstripped.) Rameau's nephew is a jester, a fool, but the richness of the book lies in its subtle suggestions that he may be a kind of frustrated genius, possibly more talented than his uncle.

From this character flows much of the psychological flamboyance and acuity of Stendhal, Dostoevsky, Hamsun, Conrad, Italo Svevo, Ralph Ellison's *Invisible Man*, and *Wittgenstein's Nephew*, in which Thomas Bernhard, following Diderot, raises the possibility that Paul Wittgenstein, the famous philosopher's nephew, was a greater philosopher than his uncle precisely because he did not write his philosophy down.

90

Look at what Stendhal does with this inheritance in *The Red and the Black*, published in 1830: Julien Sorel is strikingly unpredictable. Like Diderot's Rameau, Julien seethes with satiric callousness, self-interested impropriety, and gratuitous resentments. He is determined to make Madame de Rênal love him not out of any natural impulse but in the proud belief that this is how to conquer society, and how to repay the slights he feels she has given him: "Julien said to himself, What do I know of this woman's character? Only this—before I went away, I took hold of her hand and she withdrew it; today I withdraw my hand and she takes hold of it and presses it. There's a fine opportunity of paying her back all the contempt she has felt for me. Heaven knows how many lovers she's had. Possibly she only decided to favour me because it's so easy for us to meet."*

Stendhal's superb addition to this complex creature is subtly to reveal that, whatever he may say to himself, Julien is actually, unconsciously, in love with Madame de Rênal. (This is the kind of *novelistic* psychological subtlety not easily available to Diderot's dialogue form.) Julien is an uncannily wise portrait because he is in fact nobler than his egotism. His mantra is "Each man for himself in this desert of egoism men call life," a suitably French cynicism. But he can't actually live like this. He is too passionate, too noble. Like Diderot's Rameau, he reveres Tartuffe. But he is nothing like as brilliantly intelligent or all-seeing as the Rameau character, and this is Stendhal's great, novelistic enrichment.

---

*And it is no accident that this leap forward in characterization is accompanied by great technical developments: Stendhal's loose, relaxed, chatty kind of writing allows him to write a kind of interior monologue that is very close to stream of consciousness; one passage of this kind of narration, fairly late in the novel, continues for four pages without interruption.

Julien poses as a fearsome truth-teller, but he is just an intelligent, undereducated romantic provincial who is not quite clever or supple enough, his mind full of blowsy Napoleonic ardor. We, the readers, can see this. His understanding fluctuates; occasionally he sees clearly, but more often he cannot read upper-class society's codes as well as he thinks he can. He is proudly hypocritical, but not always hypocritical enough to see the need to hide his obvious hypocrisy—he is always blurting out his heart to people when he should keep it closed.

91

In Paris, Julien falls in love with the highborn Mathilde, the daughter of his employer. Each lover wants to be the other's love slave; but each is also too proud for this, and simultaneously wants to be the other's master. Mathilde is romantically in love with Julien's proud exceptionalism, but feels that it would be beneath her to marry a servant; Julien loves her but is fearful of being patronized. Dostoevsky, writing between the 1840s and 1881, and a keen reader of the French, would become an even greater novelist of the workings of this kind of pride and abasement. There is a direct link from Rousseau to Diderot to Dostoevsky.

In a famous scene in *Notes from Underground*, published in 1864, the narrator, an insignificant but proudly rebellious outcast, has an encounter with an impressive-looking cavalry officer in a tavern. The officer, blocked by the narrator, casually picks him up and moves him out of the way. The narrator is humiliated, and can't sleep for his dreams of revenge. He knows that this same officer walks every day down the Nevsky Prospect. The narrator follows him, "admiring" him from a distance. He determines that he will walk in the opposite direction and that when the two men meet, he, the narrator, will not budge an inch. But whenever the encounter arrives, he panics, and moves out of the way just as the officer strides past. At night he wakes, obsessively turning over the question: "Why is it invariably I who swerves first? Why precisely me and not him?" Eventually he holds his ground, the two men brush shoulders, and the narrator is overjoyed. He returns home singing Italian arias, feeling properly avenged. But the satisfaction lasts only a few days.

Dostoevsky was the great analyst—in a sense, almost the inventor—of the psychological category that Nietzsche called *ressentiment*. Again and again, Dostoevsky shows how pride is really very close to humility, and how hate is very close to a kind of sick love, in just the way that Rameau's nephew is far more dependent on the existence of his famous uncle than he will actually admit to, or in the way that Julien both loves and hates Madame de Rênal and Mathilde. In the Nevsky Prospect anecdote, the weaker man loathes but "admires" the officer—and in a sense, loathes him *because* he admires him. His impotence has less to do with his actual circumstances than with his imaginary relation to the officer, which is one of impotent dependence. Dostoevsky would call this psychological torment the "Underground," meaning a kind of poisonous, impotent alienation, a chronic instability of self, and a vaunting pride that at any moment might unexpectedly crash into its inverse—cringing self-abasement.*

Nothing in fiction, not even in Diderot and Stendhal, quite prepares one for Dostoevsky's characters. In *The Brothers Karamazov*, for in-

---

*Dostoevsky's analysis of *ressentiment* has turned out to have great prophetic relevance for the troubles we currently find ourselves in. Terrorism, clearly enough, is the triumph of resentment (sometimes justified); and Dostoevsky's Russian revolutionaries and underground men are essentially terroristic. They dream of hard revenge on a society that seems too soft to deserve sparing. And just as the narrator of *Notes from Underground* "admires" the cavalry officer he hates, so perhaps a certain kind of Islamic fundamentalist both hates and "admires" Western secularism, and hates it because he admires it (hates it, in Dostoevsky's psychological system, *because it once did him a good turn*—gave him medicine, say, or the science that could be used to crash planes into buildings).

stance, the clownish Fyodor Pavlovich is about to enter a dining room at the local monastery. He has already acted terribly in the cell of the saintly monk, Father Zosima. Fyodor decides that he will act scandalously in the dining room also. Why? Because, he thinks to himself, "it always seems to me, when I go somewhere, that I am lower than everyone else and that they all take me for a buffoon—so let me indeed play the buffoon, because all of you, to a man, are lower than I am." And as he thinks this, he remembers being asked once why he hated a certain neighbor, to which he had replied: "He never did anything to me it's true, but I once played a most shameless nasty trick on him, and the moment I did it, I immediately hated him for it."

92

Dostoevskian character has at least three layers. On the top layer is the announced motive: Raskolnikov, say, proposes several justifications for his murder of the old woman. The second layer involves unconscious motivation, those strange inversions wherein love turns into hate and guilt expresses itself as poisonous, sickly love. Thus Raskolnikov's mad need to confess his crime to the police and to Sonia the prostitute presages

Freud's comment on the action of the superego: "In many criminals," writes Freud, "especially youthful ones, it is possible to detect a very powerful sense of guilt which existed before the crime, and is therefore not its result but its motive." Or in the case of Fyodor Karamazov and his desire to punish the neighbor to whom he was once nasty, you could say that guilt is causing him, unconsciously, to be horrible to his neighbor; his behavior recalls the quip—both funny and deadly serious—of the Israeli psychoanalyst who remarked that the Germans would never forgive the Jews for the Holocaust. The third and bottom layer of motive is beyond explanation and can only be understood religiously. These characters act like this because they want to be *known*; even if they are unaware of it, they want to reveal their baseness; they want to confess. They want to reveal the dark shamefulness of their souls, and so, without knowing quite why, they act "scandalously" and appallingly in front of others, so that people "better" than they can judge them for the wretches they are.

93

There is something deeply philosophical about Dostoevsky's analysis of human behavior, and Nietzsche and Freud were attracted to his work.

(One chapter of Dostoevsky's novella *The Eternal Husband* is entitled "Analysis.") Proust, who said that all of Dostoevsky's novels might have the one title, *Crime and Punishment*, studied him with perhaps more care than he would admit to. It is Proust who elaborates and develops the philosophical analysis of psychological motive. In Proust, you can see every element of characterization—and indeed of fiction-making itself—living happily together, as if you were watching schools of fish underneath a glass-bottomed boat. Thus, his characters are in some sense both externally seen and yet highly inward; they are "flat," but are extensively analyzed by Proust as if they were "round"; and of course the novel is so massive that their flatness gets elongated over time, and no longer seems like flatness. Proust is not afraid of caricature, and positively loves to "tag" his characters with leitmotifs, or repeated "characteristics," in a Dickensian way—as, say, Marcel's grandfather likes repeatedly to say "On guard! On guard!" and Mme Verdurin always complains of getting a headache whenever music is played. He uses this method to "fix" his characters, just as the earliest novelists did, or, nearer to his own time, as Dickens, Tolstoy, and Mann all did.

But his fiction simultaneously mounts a revolt against the tyranny of fixed, Theophrastan "characteristics." Combray is presented as a closed world in which everyone knows everyone else, and Marcel's family is seen as having a supremely secure sense——sustained largely by their system of "tagging" friends and acquaintances with leitmotifs——of what people are like. When someone informs Marcel's aunt that she has just seen a stranger in the village, she wants to send the maid over to Camus, the chemist,* to ask him who this can be: the very notion of someone not known to the family is an outrage. But as Proust puts it, "our social personality is a creation of the thoughts of other people." His characters in fact change in unexpected ways, and we must constantly adjust the optic that we use to view these people. Marcel's family is sure that they know M. Swann thoroughly; but Proust reveals that they have seen only one side of him, and the least authentic at that. Likewise, Swann falls in love with Odette, because, in part, she

---

*Am I the only reader addicted to the foolish pastime of amassing instances in which minor characters in books happen to have the names of writers? Thus Camus the chemist in Proust, and another Camus in Bernanos's *Diary of a Country Priest*, and the Pyncheons in *The House of the Seven Gables*, and Horace Updike in *Babbitt*, and Brecht the dentist in *Buddenbrooks*, and Heidegger, one of Trotta's witnesses in Joseph Roth's *The Emperor's Tomb*, and Madame Foucault in Arnold Bennett's *The Old Wives' Tale*, and Father Larkin in David Jones's *In Parenthesis*, and Count Tolstoy in *War and Peace*, and a man named Barthès in *Rousseau's Confessions*, and come to think of it, a certain Madame Rousseau in Proust . . .

reminds him of a woman in a painting; but over the course of many strenuous months, he will find that one of the dangers of love is that it encourages us to fix in our amorous minds a picture of the beloved. Sometimes these alterations are caused by the smallest gestures and revelations, and are in themselves mysterious in origin. Marcel changes his idea of M. Legrandin because he glimpses him talking animatedly to someone and bowing in a peculiar way:

> This rapid straightening-up caused a sort of tense muscular wave to ripple over Legrandin's rump, which I had not supposed to be so fleshy; I cannot say why, but this undulation of pure matter, this wholly carnal fluency devoid of spiritual significance . . . awoke my mind suddenly to the possibility of a Legrandin altogether different from the one we knew.*

Progress! In Fielding and Defoe, even in the much richer Cervantes, revelation of this altering kind occurs at the level of plot—an unexpected sister, a lost will, and so on. It does not alter our conception of a character. Don Quixote, though an infinitely deep comic *idea,* is the same kind of character at the end of the book as

---

Swann's Way ("Combray").

at the beginning. (That is why his deathbed change of heart is so disconcerting.)

94

The Russians and the French essentially set the terms of the modernist novel as it flourished in Britain and America between 1920 and 1945. You can trace the excitement of encounter in Virginia Woolf's essays, especially those written in the teens and the twenties of the century, as she discovered the new translations of the Russians into English by Constance Garnett. She put it like this in "Mr Bennett and Mrs Brown" (1923):

> After reading *Crime and Punishment* and *The Idiot*, how could any young novelist believe in "characters" as the Victorians had painted them? For the undeniable vividness of so many of them is the result of their crudity. The character is rubbed into us indelibly because its features are so few and so prominent. We are given the keyword [e.g., "I never will desert Mr. Micawber"] and then, since the keyword is astonishingly apt, our imaginations swiftly supply the rest. But what keyword could be applied to Raskolnikov, Mishkin, Stavrogin, or Alyosha? These are characters without any features at all. We go into them as we descend into some enormous cavern.

Ford Madox Ford agreed (though his master was
Flaubert). Other than Richardson, he argued in
his deliciously biased book *The English Novel*,
nothing was worthy of adult attention in English
fiction until Henry James came along. For Ford,
the serious European novel began with Diderot:

> It was to Diderot—and still more to Stendhal—that
> the Novel owes its next great step forward . . . At
> that point it became suddenly evident that the
> Novel as such was capable of being regarded as a
> means of profoundly serious and many-sided discus-
> sion and therefore as a medium of profoundly seri-
> ous investigation into the human case. It came into
> its own.

95

This new approach to character meant a new approach to form. When character is stable, form
is stable and linear—the novelist begins at the
beginning, telling us about his hero's childhood
and education, moving decisively forward into
the hero's marriage, and then toward the
dramatic crux of the book (something is wrong
with the marriage). But if character is change-
able, then why begin at the beginning? Surely
it would be more effective to begin in the
middle, and then move backward, and then

move forward, and then move backward again? This is just the kind of form Conrad would use in *Lord Jim* and *The Secret Agent*, and Ford in *The Good Soldier*. Ford, again, in his memoir of Conrad:

> What was the matter with the Novel, and the British novel in particular, was that it went straight forward, whereas in your gradual making acquaintanceship with your fellows you never do go straight forward. You meet an English gentleman at your golf club. He is beefy, full of health, the model of the boy from an English public school of the finest type. You discover, gradually, that he is hopelessly neurasthenic, dishonest in matters of small change, but unexpectedly self-sacrificing, a dreadful liar, but a most painfully careful student of Lepidoptera and, finally, from the public prints, a bigamist who was once, under another name, hammered on the Stock Exchange . . . To get such a man in fiction you could not begin at his beginning and work his life chronologically to the end. You must first get him in with a strong impression, and then work backwards and forwards over his past . . .

Is it contradictory to have defended the flatness of characters while simultaneously arguing that the novel has become a more sophisticated analyst of deep, self-divided characters? No, if one resists both Forster's idea of flatness (flatness is more interesting than he makes it out to be) and his idea of roundness (roundness is more complicated than he makes it out to be). In both cases, *subtlety* of analysis is what is important.

Form

96

Form is related to story as a crowd is related to the people in that crowd. The crowd is the sum, the shape, the outline of the people in it. Likewise, form is the sum, the shape, the outline of the stories it contains. These elements are necessarily related. A certain group of people creates a certain kind of crowd—there's an obvious difference between a cocktail party and a violent mob, or between two lovers going for a stroll and thousands of people waiting in Times Square for the New Year. Rules of scope and proportion come into play: you can't fit twenty thousand people into a sitting room, while just two people standing in Times Square on New Year's Eve would seem not only a category error but a bit forlorn. In similar ways, story is related to, and to some extent determines, form. And form to some extent determines story, just as crowds or parties can take on a life of their own, and drive the activity and mood of the individuals in that crowd. The form of an epistolary novel clearly controls and limits the kind of story that will be told (it limits the communication available to

the characters, for instance). Likewise, every
novelist knows that the decision to write in the
first person sets off a chain of narrative consequences, a calculus of benefits and losses; a formal choice has a determinative effect on the
content.

97

Modernism was born out of an understanding
that, since reality has changed, the forms of the
stories we tell about that reality must also
change. If you trust in marriage, God, the progress of history, and the solidity of character,
then the fictions you make about that reality
may take complementary forms: stories culminate in the solution of marriage; characters ex-
amine their consciences, and wrestle with moral
dilemmas; and these moral struggles are represented in finished paragraphs and stable language. Plots may be initially opaque but
culminate in clarity, and many different plots—
as in *War and Peace* and *Middlemarch*—prove to
be consolingly interrelated: human beings suc-
cessfully communicate with each other, rather as
the plots involving those human beings success-
fully communicate with each other.

But imagine that these stabilities are crum-
bling, that they are newly hard to believe in, that

faith in them has been shattered by the carnage of the Great War or the calamity of the Holocaust. The form of an artwork may then have to reflect that new uncertainty. Now human beings struggle to communicate with each other; so perhaps a familial proliferation of many plots, warmly interrelated, will suddenly seem inauthentic. History does not seem to be progressing so much as stalling, or self-immolating, so perhaps the fictions set amidst that history must break off, or sliver into fragments, rather than sail on toward marriage and harmony and a spreading consensus. Words no longer seem to connect to their referents, because the surety of meaning has been exploded; words have become like an inflated currency—empty, insultingly worthless. So words must be used differently, with less certainty perhaps, and more self-consciousness: a self-conscious difficulty. Words—as in Beckett, say—may even have to die, to lapse into silence.

98

These are just a few of the ways in which form might have to be responsive to new realities, and it is more or less what Ford Madox Ford meant when he talked about feeling the need to write lives backward and forward rather than simply

forward, as before; or what Knut Hamsun meant
when he said—around the same time as Ford—
that "I dream of a literature with characters in
which their very lack of consistency is their basic characteristic"; or what Virginia Woolf meant
when she claimed that her generation of modernist artists had to write in what might seem,
to an older generation, fragmentary, spasmodic,
"unsuccessful" forms.

99

You could say that form becomes newly important in the modern age. For both modernism
and postmodernism, form is where contemporary
anxieties, preoccupations, and pleasures are in-
scribed. The frame comes off the painting, or
the frame is itself painted over. The found object
becomes an artwork, and by implication the
artwork becomes a found object. The three-
movement musical form is invaded by four minutes and thirty-three seconds of silence. The
tidy, "safe" beginnings and endings of Dixieland
fray into the ragged, complex improvisations of
bebop. A new cultural center in Paris is turned
inside out, and wears all its mechanical systems
(wiring, air ducts, and the like) on its exterior.
Novels are published in loose-leaf form, to be
assembled at will by the reader; other fictions

dwindle to fragments, are interrupted by silence and a good deal of white space.

Of course, these are the radical, pioneering examples; most art can't be as magnificently fearless, and must occupy the space most of us live in from day to day, a mixture of obedience and a desire to escape that obedience, of conventional obligation, and a wish to escape that obligation. Jenny Offill's novel *Dept. of Speculation* is a good example of a contemporary novel that is quietly radical rather than titanically experimental—its postmodernism seems to be confidently inherited rather than strenuously seized. It may not be titanic, but it is a distinctively modern book: it belongs to, and is produced by its times—it wouldn't even resemble a "proper" novel to George Eliot or Balzac or Henry James, as Elliott Carter's music or a song by Frank Ocean would be almost unrecognizable to Schubert or Brahms.

Canny and original, it offers a nice example of form and content working in complementary relation. And it is narrated by a woman who is herself caught between obligation and the desire to throw over obligation, between convention and grand disobedience. The unnamed narrator is a youngish mother who lives in New York, and who is also an ambitious writer, committed both to her daughter and to her writing. She is struggling to find the energy and ambition for both tasks. She's happily married (at least, at first), but her plan was never to get married, because of the danger it posed to creative success and fulfilment: "I was going to be an art monster instead. Women almost never become art monsters because art monsters only concern themselves with art, never mundane things. Nabokov didn't even fold his own umbrella. Vera licked his stamps for him." She was twenty-nine when she finished her first book, and there has been no successor, and the head of the department where she teaches creative writing has a habit of reminding her of this: "Tick tock. Tick tock." (The creative clock horridly mimicking the woman's biological clock.)

The marriage deteriorates. Our narrator discovers that her husband has been having an affair. She suffers all the usual emotions—rage, shock, shame—but is determined to keep the marriage intact. She is near collapse, under terrible mental strain. She wants to check herself into a hospital but is afraid that if she does, she might not come back.

100

The plot I have described could belong to almost any conventional novel, new or older—marriage, adultery, bourgeois life, unhappiness, thwarted ambition. But the book's form is unconventional, and perfectly supports and shapes those elements of the book's content that are also somewhat unconventional. Offill's narrator speaks to us in extremely short, double-spaced paragraphs. There's a great deal of terrain between these paragraphs, and though they do ultimately create a continuous narrative, they often hang in isolation, like Lydia Davis's very short, single-paragraph stories. Some of the entries are peculiar, a little whimsical or opaque or sardonic; the narrator uses humor as a buttress against painful emotion. So the narrative is a kind of interrupted stream of consciousness, allowing, like any cleverly paced interior monologue, for a managed ratio of randomized coherence: we witness a mobile, and sometimes eccentric, mind composing a narrative before our eyes. Because the book presents itself as a kind of haphazard dispatch, we have an uncanny—quite possibly fallacious—sense of autobiography, of some kind of personal authorial "truth" being disclosed, of fiction appeasing our need for "reality hunger"— an atmosphere encouraged by our knowledge that the author, like her narrator, is a writer who has taught creative writing, that she is a mother, and that like her narrator she spent a long time working on this, her second novel (fifteen years elapsed between first and second books).

More interestingly, the novel's prismatic and discontinuous form allows Offill to dart around, and thereby to build a sense of her narrator as self-divided, full of appealing contradictions; she is the more vital because she is so many things at once. She's thin-skinned, sensitive, but also tough and very funny. She feels strongly, but she blocks feeling with sarcasm and satire. She doesn't quite know herself, but also seems to know herself perfectly:

> Three things no one has ever said about me:
> *You make it look so easy.*
> *You are very mysterious.*
> *You need to take yourself more seriously.*

So the book, like its narrator, faces in many directions at once, and shows different colors to the light. It's an account of a marriage in distress but also a song in praise of marriage. It's tartly honest about the frequent boredom and fatigue of being a parent, yet it also understands all the joys and consolations of being a parent. If it laments the work that has not been done— this woman who could have been a great "art monster"—it also embodies the work that *has* been finely done, for *Dept. of Speculation* is that archetypal modernist and postmodernist document: a successful novel about the difficulty of writing a successful novel.

And it is the novel's *form* that allows for this lovely, complex variety of elements.*

101

Plot is really just *practical form*—the form the writer creates, as he or she is creating a work of fiction (working through authorial choices having to do with who is narrating the story, how to arrange all the elements, pacing, and so on). *Moral form* is the finished outline, the significant shape *we* can discern of a plot, the sense we make of something once we are able to hold that plot in our minds. Plot is reading *Pride and Prejudice*, excited to know who will marry whom, turning each page with happy surrender, led by the knowing brilliance of the author. *Moral form* is closing that novel and seeing that it is a story

---

* The thought occurs to me that the book you are currently reading uses a similar form, for similar reasons: numbered paragraphs allow me to dart around, float an idea, return to an earlier idea, and then to contradict myself a bit later. . . . And it was a convenient way to write, because like Jenny Offill's narrator, maybe like Offill herself, I was a busy parent, with two young children (four and six when I was writing the first edition of this book in 2007). Short paragraphs allowed me to write the book in small pieces, at home, amidst family interruptions and obligations (mostly joyful).

about a woman getting a man wrong and then getting him right—a story about error and correction; or, a story about two good marriages (Elizabeth and Darcy, Jane and Bingley) and three much less good ones (Charlotte and Mr. Collins; Lydia and Wickham; Mr. and Mrs. Bennet).

Plot is reading Elena Ferrante's *My Brilliant Friend*, in the excited ignorance, subtly manipulated by Ferrante, of discovering how two intelligent girls will escape the limitations of their impoverished Neapolitan life, sure that the book's title refers to the narrator's friend. Moral form is understanding, after the fact, that *My Brilliant Friend* is in fact a singular bildungsroman, that only Elena the narrator will escape, and that the "brilliant friend" is not Elena's friend Lila, but in fact Lila's friend Elena, our narrator.

102

Put it another way: plot is reading, form is literary criticism. Form is what we are left with when plot is no longer manipulating us, but when we—as readers, as critics—are manipulating plot. The plot of *Anna Karenina* is all the events and occurrences that lead to Anna's eventual death. The form of *Anna Karenina* is the finished story about a woman who committed adultery and who is finally punished—sacrificed—for that mistake. This is the punitively judgmental form of all the major nineteenth-century novels of adultery: the woman errs, the woman must die. (Until lovely Chekhov, toward the end of that moralizing tradition, compassionately unravels the terminality of this deadly cultural fable in "The Lady and the Little Dog.") When the Russian poet Anna Akhmatova complained to Isaiah Berlin about the murderous morality of *Anna Karenina*, she was complaining about the significance of its moral form: "Why should Anna have to be killed? . . . The morality of *Anna Karenina* is the morality of Tolstoy's wife, of his Moscow aunts."*

103

In these cases, we modify our immediate experience of plot (our reading experience) by our later experiences of form (our *post hoc* literary-critical experience): reading for significance is always a negotiation between our excited discovery of the work and our comprehension of the work after the excitements of discovery have faded a bit. A sign of the modernity, or postmo-

---

* Isaiah Berlin, *Personal Impressions* (1980).

dernity, of a novel like Jenny Offill's *Dept. of Spec-*
ulation is that plot (in the sense of reading to
find out "what happens next") has been so sub-
sumed by form. Plot has *become* the form the
book takes. Crudely put, there is more literary
criticism and less discovery involved in reading
a novel like Offill's.

104

Plot is what is happening; form is what happened.

105

There's an obvious philosophical or metaphysical dimension to this idea. Many of us find it
hard to see or think about the shape of our life
stories. We live caught up in plot—the rush of
day-to-day instances, the full calendar of ap-
pointments and obligations, the coincidences
and events that are sprung on us by chance. We
live in an eternal discovery phase. Perhaps once
or twice a year, on some significant day like New
Year's Eve or a birthday, we try to reflect on the
form of our lives, about what has been and what
is to come. At those moments, we try to turn
plot (chance) into form (fate, destiny, providence,
shape). Something similar occurs at a funeral or

memorial service: we gain a reflective sense of an
entire life, now finished, we get to think about
the shape of a life. We can do so because death
has stopped that life: death has imposed its stern
type of form, a metaphysical meaning and shape.
That is what Walter Benjamin says about fiction
in his essay "The Storyteller" (1936). He argues
that classic storytelling (he means oral tales, old
fables, and suchlike) has always been structured
around death. Death guarantees the authority of
the storyteller's tale; death makes a story trans-
missible. In modern life, he continues, where
death has dropped out of daily lives and become
almost invisible, and where "information" from
the newspapers has crowded out mortal storytelling, it becomes harder and harder to tell
gravely meaningful stories.

106

So fiction—here I'm extrapolating from Walter
Benjamin—ideally offers us a power we tend to
lack in our own lives: to reflect on the form and
direction of our existence; to see the birth, development, and end of a completed life. The
novel provides us with the religious power to see
beginnings and endings. "The Lord shall pre-
serve thy going out and thy coming in," goes a
verse in Psalm 121. Godlike readers of other

people's fictional lives, we can see their going out
and their coming in, their beginnings and endings, their expansions and withdrawals. Fiction
allows this in different ways. Sometimes by scope
and size—the long, populous novel, full of many
different lives, births, and deaths. Or by com-
pression and concentration: the novella that de-
picts a single life from start to finish, as in *The
Death of Ivan Ilyich*, John Williams's *Stoner*, Denis Johnson's *Train Dreams*, Alice Munro's long
story "The Bear Came Over the Mountain,"
and the work of W. G. Sebald. Yes, even though
Sebald thought that Godlike omniscience was
impossible or unpalatable in narration, one of
the most generous gifts of his fiction (I am
thinking especially of *The Emigrants* and *Austerlitz*) is the way it allows us to regard whole
lives, to think about the shape and fate of a
finished life.

107

And form does something else, too. Recall Benjamin's uncannily prescient complaint from
1936, that true storytelling is being supplanted
by a superabundance of "information." Karl Ove
Knausgaard says much the same in the first volume of *My Struggle,* when he alleges that death
now plays a "strangely ambiguous" role in our

lives: "On the one hand, it is all around us, we are inundated by news of deaths, pictures of dead people; for death, in that respect, there are no limits, it is massive, ubiquitous, inexhaustible. But this is death as an idea, death without a body, death as thought and image, death as an intellectual concept." In a world in which the screen has replaced the window, we know more than Benjamin could possibly have foreseen about the terrible unseriousness of existence amidst futile distractions of information, the too-persuasive authority of data, the allure of rival and generally inferior forms of narrative (TV, YouTube, video games, GIFs).

108

When literature competes directly with such attractions, it tends to lose.

But think instead of literature as a site of concentration, critique, surplus—concentration *as* critique: literature as the stillness at the eye of the storm, a kind of prayerful attention. Think of fictional form as something closer to the poem than to the diary. Art insists on concentration by virtue of having form. Life, as I suggested, strikes us as essentially formless; and technology, though full of cute, discrete objects, is essentially formless too. It's protean. It's about the process

of endlessly becoming, proud of its built-in ob-
solescence. 6S is always becoming 7, 7 is becoming 8, 9, X, and so on. Technology dreams
of infinity. When video games are extolled for
being like novels—for their "fiction-making
qualities"—the emphasis is generally on the
multiplicity of options and choices, not on the
determinism of form. The game player can
choose many possibilities from endlessly
tempting menus. In the same way, the best
TV dramas are likened to the novel because
their ever-unfolding serialism—episode after
episode, season after season—is thought to
resemble the serial novels of the nineteenth
century.

Yet literary form, while of course expansive
and multifarious, can also possess a certain
negative power. It shows us where things *stop*.
It places an almost sacred border around the
artwork and says, "This is not identical with
the claims of the world. This is different from
the world. This is a space that demands a certain degree of strangeness, apartness, submis-
sion, significance." Form absorbs but can finally
resist the world, is superbly autonomous. Really,
universally, human relations stop nowhere, said
Henry James. And, he went on, "the eternal
problem of the artist is to draw a circle within

which such relations merely *appear* to stop."*
The *stopping* of an endless prolongation may be
one of form's most important virtues, the artifice by which everything earns its own perfect
justification, the artifice which charges everything inside the charmed circle with chosen
meaning.

---

* Henry James, Preface to *Roderick Hudson* (New York Edition, 1907).

Sympathy and Complexity

109

In 2006, the municipal president of Neza, a tough area of two million people on the eastern edge of Mexico City, decided that the members of his police force needed to become "better citizens." He decided that they should be given a reading list, on which could be found *Don Quixote,* Juan Rulfo's beautiful novella *Pedro Páramo*, Octavio Paz's essay on Mexican culture *The Labyrinth of Solitude*, García Márquez's *One Hundred Years of Solitude*, and works by Carlos Fuentes, Antoine de Saint-Exupéry, Agatha Christie, and Edgar Allan Poe.*

Neza's chief of police, Jorge Amador, believes that reading fiction will enrich his officers in at least three ways.

> First, by allowing them to acquire a wider vocabulary . . . Next, by granting officers the opportunity to acquire experience by proxy. "A police officer

---

*See "Words on the Street," by Angel Gurria-Quintana, in *Financial Times*, March 3, 2006. I am grateful to Norman Rush for drawing my attention to this article.

must be worldly, and books enrich people's experience indirectly." Finally, Amador claims, there is an ethical benefit. "Risking your life to save other people's lives and property requires deep convictions. Literature can enhance those deep convictions by allowing readers to discover lives lived with similar commitment. We hope that contact with literature will make our police officers more committed to the values they have pledged to defend."

How quaintly antique this sounds. Nowadays, the cult of authenticity asserts that nothing is more worldly—more in the world—than police work; thousands of movies and television shows bow to this dogma. The idea that the police might get as much or more reality from their armchairs, with their noses in novels, no doubt strikes many as heretically paradoxical.

One does not have to be as morally prescriptive* as the Mexican police chief to feel that he has taxonomized three aspects of the experience

---

*We don't read *in order* to benefit in this way from fiction. We read fiction because it pleases us, moves us, is beautiful, and so on—because it is alive and we are alive. It is amusing to watch evolutionary psychology tie itself up in circularities when trying to answer the question "Why do humans spend so much time reading fiction when this yields no obvious evolutionary benefits?" The answers tend either to be utilitarian—we read in order to find out about our fellow citizens, and this has a Darwinian utility—or circular: we read because fiction pushes certain pleasure buttons.

of reading fiction: language, the world, and the extension of our sympathies toward other selves. George Eliot, in her essay on German realism, put it like this: "The greatest benefit we owe to the artist, whether painter, poet, or novelist, is the extension of our sympathies . . . Art is the nearest thing to life; it is a mode of amplifying experience and extending our contact with our fellow-men beyond the bounds of our personal lot."*

Since Plato and Aristotle, fictional and dramatic narrative has provoked two large, recurring discussions: one is centered on the question of mimesis and the real (what should fiction represent?), and the other on the question of sympathy, and how fictional narrative exercises it. Gradually, these two recurrent discussions merge, and one finds that from, say, Samuel Johnson on, it is a commonplace that sympathetic identification with characters is in some way dependent on fiction's true mimesis: to see a world and its fictional people truthfully may expand our capacity for sympathy in the actual world. It is no accident that the novel's rise in the mid-eighteenth century coincides with the rise of the philosophical discussion of sympathy, especially in thinkers like Adam Smith and Lord

---

*"The Natural History of German Life" (1856).

Shaftesbury. Smith, in *The Theory of Moral Senti-ments* (1759), argues what is merely axiomatic today, that "the source of our fellow-feeling for the misery of others" is mobilized by "changing places in fancy with the sufferer"—by putting ourselves in the other's shoes.

Tolstoy writes about this in *War and Peace.* Before Pierre is taken prisoner by the French, he has had a tendency to see people as hazy groups rather than as particularized individuals, and to feel that he has little free will. After his near-death at their hands (he thinks he is going to be executed), people come alive for him—and he comes alive to himself: "This legitimate pecu-liarity of each individual, which used to excite and irritate Pierre, now became a basis of the sympathy he felt for, and the interest he took in, other people."*

110

Ian McEwan's *Atonement* is explicitly about the dangers of failing to put oneself in someone else's shoes. The young heroine, Briony, fails in this way in the novel's first section when she wrongly convinces herself that Robbie Turner is a rapist. But putting oneself in another's shoes

---

*Book 4, Part 4, Chapter 13.

is what McEwan is signally trying to do as a
novelist in this same section, carefully inhabiting one character's point of view after another.
Briony's mother, Emily Tallis, stricken with a
migraine, lies in bed and thinks anxiously
about her children, yet the reader cannot but
notice that she is in fact a very bad imaginative
sympathizer, because her anxiety and anger get
in the way of her sympathy. Reflecting on her
daughter Cecilia's time at Cambridge, she
thinks about her own comparative lack of education, and then quickly, but unwittingly, gets
resentful:

> When Cecilia came home in July with her finals'
> result—the nerve of the girl to be disappointed with
> it!—she had no job or skill and still had a hus-
> band to find and motherhood to confront, and what
> would her bluestocking teachers—the ones with
> silly nicknames and "fearsome" reputations—have
> to tell her about that? Those self-important women
> gained local immortality for the blandest, the
> most timid of eccentricities—walking a cat on a
> dog's lead, riding about on a man's bike, being
> seen with a sandwich in the street. A generation
> later these silly, ignorant ladies would be long
> dead and still revered at High Table and spoken of
> in lowered voices.

In Adam Smith's terms, Emily is quite unable to "change places" with her daughter; in a novelist's or actor's language, she is no good at "being" Cecilia. But of course McEwan is himself wonderfully good here at "being" Emily Tallis, using free indirect style with perfect poise to inhabit her complicated envy.

Later in the section, as Emily sits by the light, she sees moths drawn to it, and recalls being told by "a professor of some science or another" that

> it was the visual impression of an even deeper darkness beyond the light that drew them in. Even though they might be eaten, they had to obey the instinct that made them seek out the darkest place, on the far side of the light—and in this case it was an illusion. It sounded to her like sophistry, or an explanation for its own sake. How could anyone presume to know the world through the eyes of an insect?

Emily *would* think this.

McEwan knowingly alludes to a celebrated dilemma in the philosophy of consciousness, most famously raised by Thomas Nagel in his essay "What Is It Like to Be a Bat?" Nagel concludes that a human cannot change places with a bat, that imaginative transfer on the part of a human is impossible: "Insofar as I can imagine this (which is not very far), it tells me only what it would be like for *me* to behave as a bat behaves. But that is not the question. I want to know what it is like for a *bat* to be a bat."* Standing up for novelists, as it were, J. M. Coetzee in his eponymous novel has his novelist-heroine, Elizabeth Costello, explicitly reply to Nagel. Costello says that imagining what it is like to be a bat would simply be the definition of a good novelist. I can imagine being a corpse, says Costello, why can I not then imagine being a bat? (Tolstoy, again, in an electrifying moment at the end of his novella *Hadji Murad*, imagines what it might be like to have one's head cut off, and for consciousness to persist for a second or two in the brain even as the head has left the body. His imaginative insight foreshadows modern neuroscience, which does indeed suggest that consciousness can continue for a minute or two in a severed head.)

111

The philosopher Bernard Williams was exercised by the inadequacy of moral philosophy.†

---

*"What Is It Like to Be a Bat?" in *Mortal Questions* (1974).
†See, especially, *Problems of the Self* (1973), *Moral Luck* (1981), and *Making*

He found that much of it, descending from Kant, essentially wrote the messiness of the self out of philosophical discussion. Philosophy, he thought, tended to view conflicts as conflicts of beliefs that could be easily solved, rather than as conflicts of desires that are not so easily solved. One example he used, in his book *Moral Luck*, was that of a man who has promised his father, after his father's death, that he will support a favored charity with his inheritance. But the son finds that, as time goes on, there is not enough money for him to fulfill his promise to his father and also look after his own children. A certain kind of moral philosopher, wrote Williams, would decide that one way to resolve this conflict is to say that the son had good reason to assume, as a tacit condition of the inheritance, that he should give money to the charity only after more immediate pressing concerns, like his children, were taken care of. The conflict is resolved by nullifying one of its elements.

Williams thought that Kantians had a tendency to treat all conflicts of obligation like this, whereas Williams was interested in what he called "tragic dilemmas," in which someone is faced with two conflicting moral requirements, each equally pressing. Agamemnon either be-

Sense of Humanity (1995).

trays his army or sacrifices his daughter; either action will cause him lasting regret and shame. For Williams, moral philosophy needed to attend to the actual fabric of emotional life, instead of talking about the self, in Kantian terms, as consistent, principled, and universal. No, said Williams, people are inconsistent; they make up their principles as they go along; and they are determined by all kinds of things—genetics, upbringing, society, and so on.

Williams often returned to Greek tragedy and epic for examples of great stories in which we see the self struggling with what he called "one-person conflicts." Curiously, he rarely if ever talked about the novel, perhaps because the novel tends to present such tragic conflicts less starkly, less tragically, in softened forms. Yet these softer conflicts are not the less interesting or profound for being softer: consider—just to pluck one kind of struggle—what extraordinary empirical insight the novel has given us into marriage and all its conflicts, both two-person (between spouses) and one-person (the lonely individual suffering inside a loveless or mistaken union). Consider *To the Lighthouse*, so moving in part because it is an account not of a brilliantly successful marriage nor of an incandescently failed one, but of an adequate one, in which struggles and little compromises are daily enacted. Here, Mr. and Mrs. Ramsay walk in the garden and talk about their son:

> They paused. He wished Andrew could be induced to work harder. He would lose every chance of a scholarship if he didn't. "Oh, scholarships!" she said. Mr Ramsay thought her foolish for saying that, about a serious thing, like a scholarship. He should be very proud of Andrew if he got a scholarship, he said. She would be just as proud of him if he didn't, she answered. They disagreed always about this, but it did not matter. She liked him to believe in scholarships, and he liked her to be proud of Andrew whatever he did.

The subtlety lies in the picture of each side disagreeing, but wanting nonetheless the other to remain the same.

Of course, the novel does not provide philosophical answers (as Chekhov said, it only needs to ask the right questions). Instead, it does what Williams wanted moral philosophy to do—it gives the best account of the complexity of our moral fabric. When Pierre, in *War and Peace*, begins to change his ideas about himself and other people, he realizes that the only way to understand people properly is to see things from each person's point of view: "There was a new feature in Pierre's relations with Willarski, with the princess, with the doctor, and with all the people he now met, which gained for him the general goodwill. This was his acknowledgement of the impossibility of changing a man's convictions by words, and his recognition of the possibility of everyone thinking, feeling, and seeing things each from his own point of view . . . The difference, and sometimes complete contradiction, between men's opinions and their lives, and between one man and another, pleased him and evoked from him an amused and gentle smile."*

---

*Book 4, Part 4, Chapter 13.

Language

112

The poet Glyn Maxwell likes to conduct the following test in his writing classes, one apparently used by Auden. He gives them Philip Larkin's poem "The Whitsun Weddings," with certain words blacked out. He tells them what kinds of words—nouns, verbs, adjectives—have been omitted, and how they complete the meter of the line. The aspiring poets must try to fill in the blanks. Larkin is traveling by train from the north of England to London, and as he watches from the window, he records passing sights. One of these is a hothouse, which he renders: "A hothouse flashed uniquely." Maxwell excises "uniquely," telling his students that a trisyllabic adverb is missing. Not once has a student supplied "uniquely." "Uniquely" is unique.

113

Nietzsche laments, in *Beyond Good and Evil*: "What a torment books written in German are for him who has a *third ear*." If prose is to be as well written as poetry, novelists and readers must

develop their own third ears. We have to read
musically, testing the precision and rhythm of a
sentence, listening for the almost inaudible rustle of historical association clinging to the hems
of modern words, attending to patterns, repeti-
tions, echoes, deciding why one metaphor is successful and another is not, judging how the
perfect placement of the right verb or adjective
seals a sentence with mathematical finality. We
must proceed on the assumption that almost all
prose popularly acclaimed as beautiful ("she
writes like an angel") is nothing of the sort, that
almost every novelist will at some point be base-
lessly acclaimed for writing "beautifully" as almost all flowers are at some point acclaimed for
smelling nice.

114

There is a way in which even complex prose is
quite simple—because of that mathematical finality by which a perfect sentence cannot admit
of an infinite number of variations, cannot be extended without aesthetic blight: its perfection
is the solution to its own puzzle; it could not be
done better.

There is a familiar American simplicity, for
instance, which is Puritan and colloquial in origin, "a sort of ecstatic fire that takes things down

to the essentials," as Marilynne Robinson has it in her novel *Gilead*. We recognize it in the Puritan sermon, in Jonathan Edwards, in Ulysses S. Grant's memoirs, in Mark Twain, in Willa Cather, in Hemingway. These are the obvious examples. But that same simplicity is also always present in much more ornate writers like Melville, Emerson, Cormac McCarthy. The stars "fall all night in bitter arcs." "The horses stepped archly among the shadows that fell over the road." These lucid phrases are from McCarthy's *Blood Meridian* and *All the Pretty Horses*, respectively, books whose prose is often fantastically baroque. Marilynne Robinson's novel *Gilead* achieves an almost holy simplicity; but this is the same writer whose earlier novel, *Housekeeping*, abounds in complicated Melvillean metaphor and analogy. Is the following passage from *Gilead* an example of simple or complicated prose?

This morning a splendid dawn passed over our house on its way to Kansas. This morning Kansas rolled out of its sleep into a sunlight grandly announced, proclaimed throughout heaven—one more of the very finite number of days that this old prairie has been called Kansas, or Iowa. But it has all been one day, that first day. Light is constant, we just turn over in it. So every day is in fact the self-same evening and morning. My grandfather's grave

turned into the light, and the dew on his weedy
little mortality patch was glorious.

Weedy little mortality patch—how fine that is.

115

Prose is always simple *in this sense*, because
language is the ordinary medium of daily
communication—unlike music or paint. Our ordinary possessions are being borrowed by even
very difficult writers: the millionaires of style—
difficult, lavish stylists like Sir Thomas Browne,
Melville, Ruskin, Lawrence, James, Woolf—are
very prosperous, but they use the same banknotes
as everyone else. "Vague squares of rich colour"
is the simple little formulation Henry James
uses to describe Old Master paintings seen from
a distance in a darkened room in *The Portrait of
a Lady*. How precise, paradoxically, is that
"vague"! Aren't these exactly the best words in
the best order? "The day waves yellow with all
its crops." That is Woolf, from *The Waves*. I am
consumed by this sentence, partly because I cannot quite explain why it moves me so much. I
can see, hear, its beauty, its strangeness. Its music
is very simple. Its words are simple. And its
meaning is simple, too. Woolf is describing the
sun rising and finally filling the day with its yel-

low fire. The sentence means something like: this is what a field of corn on a summer's day will look like when everything is blazing with sunlight—a yellow semaphore, a sea of moving color. We *know* exactly and instantly what Woolf means, and we think: That could not be put any better. The secret lies in the decision to avoid the usual image of crops waving, and instead, to write "the day waves": the effect is suddenly that the day itself, the very fabric and temporality of the day, seems saturated in yellow. And then that peculiar, apparently nonsensical "waves yellow" (how can anything wave yellow?), conveys a sense that yellowness has so intensely taken over the day itself that it has taken over our verbs, too—yellowness has conquered our agency. How do we wave? We wave yellow. That is all we can do. The sunlight is so absolute that it stuns us, makes us sluggish, robs us of will. Eight simple words evoke color, high summer, warm lethargy, ripeness.

116

In *Sea and Sardinia*, Lawrence describes the short legs of King Victor Emmanuel; but he refers to "his little short legs." Now, in some technical sense, there is no need to have both "short" and "little" in the same sentence. If Lawrence were a schoolboy, his teacher would write "redundant" in the margin and remove one of the adjectives. But say it aloud a few times, and it suddenly seems inevitable. We need the two words, because they sound farcical together. And short does not mean the same as little: the two words enjoy each other's company; and "little short legs" is more original than "short little legs," because it is jumpier, is more absurd, forcing us to stumble slightly—stumble short-leggedly—over the unexpected rhythm.

117

We cannot write about rhythm and not refer to Flaubert. Of course writers before him had agonized about style. But no novelist agonized as much or as publicly, no novelist fetishized the poetry of "the sentence" in the same way, no novelist pushed to such an extreme the potential alienation of form and content (Flaubert longed to write what he called a "book about nothing"). And no novelist before Flaubert reflected as self-consciously on questions of technique. With Flaubert, literature became "essentially problematic," as one scholar puts it.*

Or just modern? Flaubert himself affected a

---

*Stephen C. Heath, in *Flaubert: Madame Bovary* (1998).

nostalgia for the great unself-conscious writers who came before him, the beasts of instinct who just got on with it, like Molière and Cervantes; they, said Flaubert in his letters, "had no techniques." He, on the other hand, was betrothed to "atrocious labor" and "fanaticism." This fanaticism was applied to the music and rhythm of the sentence. In different ways, the modern novelist is shadowed by that monkish labor. It is a difficult inheritance, in some ways imprisoning, and we must escape it. The rich stylist (the Bellow, the Updike) is made newly self-conscious about his richness; but the plainer stylist (Hemingway, for example) has also become self-conscious about his plainness, itself now resembling a form of highly controlled and minimalist richness, a stylishness of renunciation. The realist feels Flaubert breathing down his neck: Is it well written enough? But the formalist or postmodernist is also indebted to Flaubert for the dream of a book about nothing, a book flying high on style alone. (Alain Robbe-Grillet and Nathalie Sarraute, originators of the *nouveau roman*, were explicit about crediting Flaubert as their great precursor.)

Flaubert loved to read aloud. It took him thirty-two hours to read his overblown lyrical fantasia, *The Temptation of Saint Anthony*, to two friends. And when he dined in Paris at the

Goncourts', he loved to read out examples of bad writing. Turgenev said that he knew of "no other writer who scrupled in quite that way." Even Henry James, the master stylist, was somewhat appalled by the religious devotion with which Flaubert assassinated repetition, unwanted clichés, clumsy sonorities. The scene of his writing has become notorious: the study at Croisset, the slow river outside the window, while inside the bearish Norman, wrapped in his dressing gown and wreathed in pipe smoke, groaned and complained about how slow his progress was, each sentence laid as slowly and agonizingly as a fuse.*

So what did Flaubert mean by style, by the music of a sentence? This, from *Madame Bovary*—Charles is stupidly proud that he has got Emma pregnant: "L'idée d'avoir engendré le délectait." So compact, so precise, so rhythmic. Literally, this is "The idea of having engendered

---

*Though one wonders if a great deal of time was not spent just sleeping and masturbating (Flaubert likened sentences to ejaculate). Often, the excruciation of the stylist seems to be a front for writer's block. This was the case with the marvelous American writer J. F. Powers, for instance, of whom Sean O'Faolain joked, in Wildean fashion, that he "spent the morning putting in a comma and the afternoon wondering whether or not he should replace it with a semicolon." More usual, I think, is the kind of literary routine ascribed to the minor English writer A. C. Benson—that he did nothing all morning and then spent the afternoon writing up what he'd done in the morning.

delighted him." Geoffrey Wall, in his Penguin translation, renders it as: "The thought of having impregnated her was delectable to him." This is good, but pity the poor translator. The translation is a wan cousin of the French. Say the French out loud, as Flaubert would have done, and you encounter four "ay" sounds in three of the words: "l'idée, engendré, délectait." An English translation that tried to mimic the untranslatable music of the French—that tried to mimic the rhyming—would sound like bad hip-hop: "The notion of procreation was a delectation."

118

Yet even if Flaubertianism casts a permanent shadow over the development of style in fiction, our sense of what is musical in style constantly changes. Flaubert feared repetition, but of course Hemingway and Lawrence would make repetition the basis of their most beautiful effects. Here is Lawrence, again, in *Sea and Sardinia*:

> Very dark under the great carob tree as we go down
> the steps. Dark still the garden. Scent of mimosa,
> and then of jasmine. The lovely mimosa tree invis-
> ible. Dark the stony path. The goat whinnies out of
> her shed. The broken Roman tomb which lolls right

over the garden track does not fall on me as I slip
under its massive tilt. Ah dark garden, dark garden,
with your olives and your wine, your medlars and
mulberries and many almond trees, your steep ter-
races ledged high up above the sea, I am leaving
you, slinking out. Out between the rosemary
hedges, out of the tall gate, on to the cruel steep
stony road. So under the dark, big eucalyptus trees,
over the stream, and up towards the village. There,
I have got so far.

Lawrence is leaving a Sicilian house at dawn, and
heading for the ferry: "I am leaving you, slinking out." This is his farewell to all that he has
loved there. The passage might as well be an
example of simplicity as of musicality. Its complexity, such as it is, lies in his attempt to use
his prose to register, minute by minute, the
painful largo of this farewell. Each sentence
slows down to make its own farewell: "Scent of
mimosa, and then of jasmine. The lovely mimosa tree invisible." First you smell the scent,
then you see—or apprehend—the tree. After
that, the path. Sentence by sentence.

And meanwhile the darkness is changing as
the day breaks, which is why Lawrence repeats
his word "dark." In fact, every time he repeats
the word, the word has changed a little, because
each time Lawrence changes what he attaches

the word "dark" to: *very dark—dark still—dark the—dark garden—the dark, big eucalyptus trees.* Repetition is not really repetition after all. It is alteration: dawn light is slowly dissolving this darkness. At the end of it all, the writer has done no more than get onto the path: "There, I have got so far." This could be a description of the movement of the prose, too. So near, so far. So little, so much.

119

Listen to the operation of an intensely musical ear in one of the greatest stylists of American prose, Saul Bellow, a writer who makes even the fleet-footed—the Updikes, the DeLillos, the Roths—seem like monopodes. Like all serious novelists, Bellow read poetry: Shakespeare first (he could recite lines and lines from the plays, remembered from his schooldays in Chicago), then Milton, Keats, Wordsworth, Hardy, Larkin, and his friend John Berryman. And behind all this, with its English stretching all the way back into deeper antiquity, the King James Bible. A river, seen as "crimped, green, blackish, glassy," or Chicago as "blue with winter, brown with evening, crystal with frost," or New York as "sheer walls, gray spaces, dry lagoons of tar and pebbles." Here is a paragraph from his story

"The Old System," in which Isaac Braun, in a high state of agitation, rushes to get his plane at Newark airport.

> On the airport bus, he opened his father's copy of the Psalms. The black Hebrew letters only gaped at him like open mouths with tongues hanging down, pointing upward, flaming but dumb. He tried—forcing. It did no good. The tunnel, the swamps, the auto skeletons, machine entrails, dumps, gulls, sketchy Newark trembling in fiery summer, held his attention minutely . . . Then in the jet running with concentrated fury to take off— the power to pull away from the magnetic earth; and more: When he saw the ground tilt backward, the machine rising from the runway, he said to himself in clear internal words, "*Shema Yisrael*," Hear, O Israel, God alone is God! On the right, New York leaned gigantically seaward, and the plane with a jolt of retracted wheels turned toward the river. The Hudson green within green, and rough with tide and wind. Isaac released the breath he had been holding, but sat belted tight. Above the marvelous bridges, over clouds, sailing in atmosphere, you know better than ever that you are no angel.

Bellow had a habit of writing repeatedly about flying, partly, I guess, because it was the great

obvious advantage he had over his dead compet-
itors, those writers who had never seen the
world from above the clouds: Melville, Tolstoy,
Proust. He does it very well. Notice, first of all,
that the rhythm of the passage never settles
down. Bellow gets a list going, with a repeated
"the," and then suddenly drops "the" halfway
through: "*The* tunnels, *the* swamps, *the* auto skel-
etons, / machine entrails, dumps, gulls, sketchy
Newark . . ." The effect is destabilizing, agitat-
ing. (Thus even this passage is a version of free
indirect style, striving to capture or mimic Isaac
Braun's flustered anxiety, his eye failing to retain
things seen through the bus window.) And in
sentence after sentence the world is captured
with brimming novelty: Newark seen as
"sketchy" and "trembling in fiery summer," the
jet "running with concentrated fury to take off"
(a phrase that with its unpunctuated onrush itself enacts such a concentrated fury), New York
which, as the plane tilts, "leaned gigantically
seaward" (say the phrase aloud, and see how
the words themselves—"leaned gi-gan-tic-ally
sea-ward"—elongate the experience, so that the
very language embodies the queasiness it describes); the dainty, unexpected rhythm of "The
Hudson green within green, and rough with
tide and wind" ("green within green" captures

very precisely the different shades of green that we see in large bodies of cold water when several thousand feet above them); and finally, "sailing in atmosphere"—isn't that exactly what the freedom of flight feels like? And yet until this moment one did not have these words to fit this feeling. Until this moment, one was comparatively inarticulate; until this moment, one had been blandly inhabiting a deprived eloquence.

How does this kind of stylishness avoid the dilemma we explored earlier, in Flaubert and Updike and David Foster Wallace, in which the stylish novelist uses words that his more hapless fictional character could never have come up with? It doesn't. The tension is still there, and Bellow has to remind us that Newark "held his [Isaac's] attention minutely," as if to say, "you see, Isaac really is looking as hard as I am at these things." But Bellow's details and rhythms are so mobile, so dynamic, that they seem less vulnerable to the charge of aestheticism than do Flaubert's or Updike's. That smooth, premade wall of prose that Flaubert wanted us to gasp at— "How does it all come about?"—is here a rougher lattice, through which we seem to see a style apparently in the process of being made. This roughened-up texture and rhythm is, for me at least, one of the reasons that I rarely find Bel-

low an intrusive lyricist, despite his high stylishness.*

120

One way to tell slick genre prose from really interesting writing is to look, in the former case,
for the absence of different registers. An efficient
thriller will often be written in a style that is
locked into place: the musical analogue of this
might be a tune, proceeding in unison, the mel-
ody separated only by octave intervals, without
any harmony in the middle. By contrast, rich
and daring prose avails itself of harmony and
dissonance by being able to move in and out of
place. In writing, a "register" is nothing more
than a name for a kind of diction, which is nothing more than a name for a certain, distinctive
way of saying something—so we talk about
"high" and "low" registers (e.g., the highish
"Father" and the lower "Pop"), grand and vernacular diction, mock-heroic diction, clichéd registers, and so on.

We have a conventional expectation that prose

---

*Lukács, in *Studies in European Realism*, distinguishes between the frozen
detail of Flaubert and Zola, and the more dynamic detail of Tolstoy,
Shakespeare, and Balzac. Lukács borrowed this idea from Lessing's *Lao-
coön*, in which Lessing praises Homer's description of Achilles' shield, not
as something finished and complete, but "as a shield that is being made."

should be written in only one unvarying
register—a solid block, like everyone agreeing
to wear black at a funeral. But this is a social
convention, and eighteenth-century prose, for
instance, is especially good at subverting this
expectation, wringing comedy out of the jostling
together of different registers that we had not
thought should share the same family space. We
saw how well Jane Austen made fun of Sir William Lucas, by writing that he built a new house,
"denominated from that period Lucas Lodge."
With the phrase "denominated from that period," and especially the fancy verb "denominated," Austen uses a grand register (or pompous
diction) to mock Sir William's own pomposity.
More subtly, in *Emma*, Mrs. Elton, on the trip
to Donwell Abbey to pick strawberries, is described as dressed in "all her apparatus of happiness, her large bonnet and her basket." The
phrase "apparatus of happiness" is of course absolutely killing, and, as in the Lucas Lodge passage, the comedy emanates from the little lift in
register, the move upward, to that word "apparatus." Suggestive of technical efficiency, the
word belongs to a scientific register that puts it
at odds with "of happiness." An apparatus of
happiness sounds more like an inverted torture
machine than a bonnet and basket, and it promises a kind of doggedness, a persistence, that fits

Mrs. Elton's character, and which makes the heart sink.

Austen's tricks can be found in modern writers as different as Muriel Spark and Philip Roth. In *The Prime of Miss Jean Brodie*, one of the little girls, Jenny, is confronted one day by a flasher; or as Spark wittily has it, "was accosted by a man joyfully exposing himself beside the Water of Leith." That adverb, "joyfully," is marvelously unexpected, and seems to have no place in the sentence. It robs the incident of menace, and makes it a kind of fairy tale. The capitalized "Water of Leith" introduces an absurd mock-heroic register that Pope would have applauded. The Water of Leith is a small river; to insist on identifying it makes further fun of the incident, and the aural suggestion of Lethe is very funny. You can hear the comedy in these different dictions—and laugh—without necessarily knowing why.*

---

*It is partly by shifts in register that we gain a sense of a human *voice* speaking to us—Austen's, Spark's, Roth's. Likewise, by dancing between registers a character sounds real to us, whether Hamlet or Leopold Bloom. Movements in diction capture some of the waywardness and roominess of actual thinking: David Foster Wallace and Norman Rush exploit this to considerable effect. Rush's two novels, *Mating* and *Mortals*, are full of the most fantastic shifts in diction, and the effect is the creation of a real but strange American voice, at once overeducated and colloquial: "This jeu maintained its facetious character, but there came a time when I began to resent it as a concealed way of short-circuiting my

Philip Roth does something similar in this long sentence from *Sabbath's Theater*. Mickey Sabbath, satanic seducer and misanthrope, has been having a long, juicy affair with a Croatian-American, Drenka:

> Lately, when Sabbath suckled at Drenka's uberous breasts—uberous, the root word of *exuberant*, which is itself *ex* plus *uberare*, to be fruitful, to overflow like Juno lying prone in Tintoretto's painting where the Milky Way is coming out of her tit—suckled with an unrelenting frenzy that caused Drenka to roll her head ecstatically back and to groan (as Juno herself may have once groaned), "I feel it deep down in my cunt," he was pierced by the sharpest of longings for his late little mother.

This is an amazingly blasphemous little mélange. This sentence is really dirty, and partly because it conforms to the well-known definition of dirt—matter out of place, which is itself a definition of the mixing of high and low dictions. But why would Roth engage in such baroque deferrals and shifts? Why write it so complicatedly? If you render the simple matter of his sen-

---

episode of depression, because he preferred me to be merry, naturally."
Or: "I was manic and global. Everything was a last straw. I went up the hill on passivity and down again."

tence and keep everything in place—i.e., remove the jostle of registers—you see why. A simple version would go like this: "Lately, when Sabbath sucked Drenka's breasts, he was pierced by the sharpest of longings for his late mother." It is still funny, because of the slide from lover to mother, but it is not *exuberant*. So the first thing the complexity achieves is to enact the exuberance, the hasty joy and chaotic desire, of sex. Second, the long, mock-pedantic, suspended subclause about the Latin origin of "uberous" and Tintoretto's painting of Juno works, in proper music-hall fashion, to delay the punchline of "he was pierced by the sharpest of longings for his late little *mother*." (It also delays, and makes more shocking and unexpected, the entrance of "cunt.") Third, since the comedy of the subject matter of the sentence involves moving from one register to another—from a lover's breast to a mother's—it is fitting that the style of the sentence mimics this scandalous shift, by engaging in its own stylistic shifts, going up and down like a manic EKG: so we have "suckled" (high diction), "breasts" (medium), *"uberare"* (high), "Tintoretto's painting" (high), "where the Milky Way is coming out of her tit" (low), "unrelenting frenzy" (high, rather formal diction), "as Juno herself may have once groaned" (still quite high), "cunt" (very low), "pierced by the

sharpest of longings" (high, formal diction
again). By insisting on equalizing all these different levels of diction, the style of the sentence
works as style should, to incarnate the meaning,
and the meaning itself, of course, is all about the
scandal of equalizing different registers. *Sabbath's
Theater* is a passionate, intensely funny, repellent,
and very moving portrait of the scandal of male
sexuality, which is repeatedly linked in the book
to vitality itself. To be able to have an erection
in the morning, to be able to seduce women in
one's mid-sixties, to be able to persist in scan-
dalizing bourgeois morality, to be able to say
every single day, as the aging Mickey does, "Fuck
the laudable ideologies!" is to be alive. And this
sentence is utterly alive, and is alive by virtue of
the way it scandalizes proper norms. Is it Drenka
or Juno or Mickey's late mother who is being
fucked in this sentence? All three of them. Roth
brilliantly catches the needy, babyish side of
male sexuality, in which a lover's breast is still
really mommy's suckling tit, because mommy
was your first and only lover. Drenka, then, in-
evitably, is both Madonna (mother, Juno) and
whore (because she can't be as good as mommy
was). In classic misogynistic fashion, the woman
is adored and hated by men because she is the
source of life—the Milky Way flows out of her
breasts, and children come from between her

legs ("the Monster of the Beginning Womb," as
Allen Ginsberg calls it in *Kaddish*). Men cannot
rival that, even as they, like Mickey or late Yeats,
rage on about male "vitality." And notice the
subtle way that, with his verb "pierced" ("pierced
by the sharpest of longings"), Roth inverts the
presumed male-female order. Mickey, who is
presumably *piercing* (in a sexual sense) this
mother-whore by *entering* her, is really being
pierced or entered—fucked back in turn—by the
woman who gave birth to him. All this in one
superb sentence.

121

Metaphor is analogous to fiction, because it floats
a rival reality. It is the entire imaginative process in one move. If I compare the slates on a roof
to an armadillo's back, or—as I did earlier—the
bald patch on the top of my head to a crop circle (or on very bad days, to the kind of flattened
ring of grass that a helicopter's blades make
when it lands in a field), I am asking you to do
what Conrad said fiction should make you do—
see. I am asking you to imagine another dimension, to picture a likeness. Every metaphor or
simile is a little explosion of fiction within the
larger fiction of the novel or story. Near the end
of *The Rainbow*, Ursula looks out at London from

her hotel balcony. It is dawn, and "the lamps of Picadilly, stringing away beside the trees of the park, were becoming pale and moth-like." Pale and moth-like! We know, in a flash, exactly what Lawrence means, but we had not *seen* those lights like moths until this moment.

And of course this explosion of fiction-within-fiction is not exclusively visual, any more than detail in fiction is exclusively visual. "As he spoke he stroked both sides of his mutton-chop whiskers as if he wished to caress simultaneously both halves of the monarchy." That is from Joseph Roth's novel *The Radetzky March*, which chronicles the decline of a family in the last years of the Austro-Hungarian empire. The two halves of the monarchy, then, are the Austrian side and the Hungarian side. It is a fantastical image, excitingly surreal and strange, but you could not say that the simile brings the two halves of the whiskers to our eye, any more than Shakespeare (or his cowriter) intends us to visualize something when a fisherman in *Pericles* exclaims: "Here's a fish hangs in the net, like a poor man's right in the law." Instead, Roth's is the kind of hypothetical or analogical—"as if"—metaphor that Shakespeare is very fond of. It wittily tells us something about the devotion of this Hapsburg bureaucrat; it arrests him in an outlandishly symbolic gesture.

122

Wittgenstein once complained that Shakespeare's similes were "*in the ordinary sense*, bad."*
Doubtless he meant Shakespeare's fondness for metaphorical extravagance, and his tendency to mix his metaphors, as when Henry complains about "the moody frontier of a servant brow" in *Henry IV, Part 1.* There are readers who will object that a brow cannot be a frontier, and that a frontier cannot be moody. But again, as in the Lawrence example, metaphor is doing here what it is supposed to do; it is speeding us, imaginatively, toward a new meaning. A better example—also involving a brow—occurs in *Macbeth*, when Macbeth is watching his wife sleepwalking, and implores the doctor to help her: "Raze out [i.e., erase] the written troubles of the brain." Wittgenstein would not approve, but Wittgenstein was not, in the end, a very literary reader. That strange image manages to combine the idea of our trouble as a sentence of judgment, "written" by the gods; the customary idea of the mind as a book upon which are written our thoughts; and the idea of the lines on a troubled brow, lines written into the brow by distress. Readers and theatergoers storm upon

---

Culture and Value, edited by G. H. Von Wright and Heikki Nyman, translated by Peter Winch (1980). The italics are Wittgenstein's.

these meanings in a flash, without having to un-pack them in the laborious way I have just done.

Actually, there is a way in which mixed meta-phor is perfectly logical, and not an aberration at all. After all, metaphor is already a mixing of disparate agents—a brow is not really like a frontier—and so mixed metaphor can be said to be the essence, the hypostasis, of metaphor: if a brow can be like a frontier, it follows that a fron-tier can be moody. In contemporary parlance, what people dislike about mixed metaphor is that it tends to combine two different *clichés*, as in, say, "out of a sea of despair, he has pulled forth a plum." The metaphorical aspect is actu-ally dimmed, almost to nonexistence, by the presence of two or more mixed clichés (which by definition are themselves dim or dead meta-phors). But Shakespeare's metaphors more often inhabit a speculative realm rather than a me-chanical one, in which readers and audience have already been asked to abandon a custom-ary world of familiar correspondence (as, for in-stance, when Macbeth likens pity to a newborn babe). Henry James was once reproved for using mixed metaphors in a novel, and he replied to his correspondent that he used not mixed but "loose metaphors": "Lastly, the metaphor about muffling shame in a splendor that asks no ques-tions is indeed a trifle mixed; but it is essentially a loose metaphor—it isn't a simile—it doesn't pretend to sail close to the wind."* (And notice that the inveterately metaphorical James has to provide another metaphor, about sailing close to the wind, to explain his own metaphors.)†

But most similes and metaphors, certainly of the visual kind, do pretend, of course, to sail close to the wind, and give us that sense that something has been newly painted before our eyes. Here, for instance, are four metaphorical descriptions of fire, all of them tremendously successful. Lawrence, seeing a fire in a grate, writes of it as "that rushing bouquet of new flames in the chimney" (*Sea and Sardinia*). Hardy describes a "scarlet handful of fire" in Gabriel Oak's cottage in *Far from the Madding Crowd*. Bellow has this sentence in his story "A Silver Dish": "The blue flames fluttered like a school of fishes in the coal fire." And Norman Rush, in his novel *Mating*, which is set in Botswana, has his hero come upon an abandoned village, where he sees that "cooking fires wagged in some of the

---

*Letter to Grace Norton, March 1876, in *Henry James: A Life in Letters*, edited by Philip Horne (1999).

†James can, when he wants to, sail close to the wind in simile, thus nicely disproving Nabokov's slanderous complaint to Edmund Wilson. In *The American Scene*, written in 1907, James likens the already crowded Manhattan skyline to a pincushion whose pins have been put in at nighttime, any old how. Later in the same book he compares it to an upturned comb, with teeth missing.

lalwapas" (a lalwapa is a kind of African court-
yard). So: a rushing bouquet (DHL); a scarlet
handful of fire (TH); a school of fishes (SB); and
a wagging fire (NM). Is one better than the
others? Each works slightly differently. The Bellow and the Lawrence are perhaps the most
visual—we can see in our mind's eye the flames
as bright as flowers and rippling like fish (notice
that Bellow writes "a school of fishes" not "a
school of fish," precisely because the plural
sounds more numerous, more rippling). Hardy
is the most homely, perhaps, but he is daring in
his way: we might think of a handful of dust but
never of a handful of fire, since we keep our
hands away from fire. Rush's is marvelous. Flame
does indeed wag (i.e., bend, flap, dip, decrease,
increase), but when would most of us ever think
to use the verb "wag"? Like Hardy's handful,
wag is daring precisely because it is a strikingly
unfiery verb. Tails wag, and jokers are called
wags, but flame belongs to a different realm
from this coziness. Lawrence's is the most ver-
bally daring, because, along with the likening of
flames to a bouquet of flowers (and of course,
flames are indeed gathered in a grate for us as a
bouquet gathers flowers in a vase), there is the
pairing of "rushing" with "bouquet"—"a rushing bouquet"—which is a further metaphor
within the larger metaphor, since while flames

can rush at us, bouquets cannot. In a way, it is a mixed metaphor. So Lawrence is the only writer in this group to give us two metaphors for the price of one. (*New* flames, to go with the idea of new flowers, perhaps introduces a third.)

These four examples tell us that often the leap toward the counterintuitive, toward the very opposite of the thing you are seeking to compare, is the secret of powerful metaphor. Flame is as far from flowers, fish, handfuls, and wagging as can be imagined. Clearly this is the principle, if not quite the effect, of the technique made famous by the Russian formalists, *ostranenie*, or defamiliarization. Céline, in his novel *Journey to the End of the Night*, shocks us out of the familiar by likening rush hour in Paris to catastrophe: "Seeing them all fleeing in that direction you'd think that there must have been some catastrophe at Argenteuil, that the town was on fire." Nabokov, showing his Symbolist and formalist roots, likens a rainbow-colored oil slick in *The Gift* to "asphalt's parakeet." Obviously, whenever you extravagantly liken x to y, and a large gap exists between x and y, you will be drawing attention to the fact that x is really nothing like y, as well as drawing attention to the effort involved in producing such extravagances.

The kind of metaphor I most delight in, however, like the ones above about fire, estranges and then instantly connects, and in doing the latter so well, hides the former. The result is a tiny shock of surprise, followed by a feeling of inevitability. In *To the Lighthouse*, Mrs. Ramsay says goodnight to her children, and carefully closes the bedroom door, and lets "the tongue of the door slowly lengthen in the lock." The metaphor in that sentence lies not so much in "tongue," which is fairly conventional (since people do talk about locks having tongues) but is secretly buried in the verb, "lengthen." That verb *lengthens* the whole procedure: Isn't this the best description you have ever read of someone very sl-o-w-ly turning a handle of a door so as not to waken children? (Tongue is good, too, because tongues make noise, while this particular tongue has to stay silent. And the now blissfully silent children have of course been using their noisy tongues all day.) In the opposite spirit, in Katherine Mansfield's "Daughters of the Late Colonel," Kate, the cook, has a habit of "bursting through the door in her usual fashion, as though she had discovered some secret panel." It would take the repetition of weekly episodes, and the full panoply of actors and set to reproduce, in Kramer's similar antics on *Seinfeld*, what Mansfield captures in one simile. Mansfield is very good at simile; in another of her stories, "The Voyage," a girl on a boat listens to her grandmother, lying in a bed above her saying her prayers, "a long, soft whispering, as though someone was gently, gently rustling among tissue paper to find something."

123

In New York City, the garbage collectors call maggots "disco rice."* That is as good as anything I have been discussing, and indeed there is a link between that kind of metaphor-making and Hardy's handful of fire, or Mansfield's grandmother saying her prayers like someone rummaging through tissue paper, or Marilynne Robinson's "weedy little mortality patch." This returns us to one of our continued questions, how the stylist manages to be a stylist without writing over his or her characters. Metaphor that is "successful" in a poetic sense but that is at the same time character-appropriate metaphor—the kind of metaphor that this particular character or community would produce—is one way of resolving the tension between author and character; we saw this when discussing the "leggy thing" of the nutcracker in *Pnin*. Shakespeare's fisherman likens a fish caught in a net to "a poor man's right hanging in the law." We might as-

---

*See Elizabeth Royte, *Garbarge Land: On the Secret Trail of Trash* (2005).

sume, by extension, that he sometimes likens
the law to a fisherman's net: he finds the image
which is near at hand. Chekhov describes a bird's
nest as looking as if someone has left a glove in
a tree—in a story about peasants. Cesare Pavese,
in *The Moon and the Bonfire*, a great novel set in
a poor, backward Italian village and its rural en-
virons, describes the moon as yellow, "like po-
lenta." In *Tess of the D'Urbervilles*, Angel and Tess
are riding in a milk cart, and the milk is slop-
ping in the pails behind them—except that
Hardy says that the milk is "clucking" in the
pails, which is first of all true to life (we can instantly hear the milk *clucking* in the pails) and is
also very homely and farmlike. (Likewise, in the
same novel he describes a cow's udder as having
teats that stick out like the short little legs on
the bottom of a Gypsy's cooking pot.) In *Loving*,
Henry Green describes a pretty housemaid's eyes
as glowing "like plums dipped in cold water"—
in a novel almost exclusively about domestic servants in a large castle. In all these cases except
the Shakespearean one, metaphor is not explicitly tied to a character. It issues forth in third-
person narration. So it seems to be produced by
the stylish, metaphor-making author, but it also
hovers around the character, and seems to emanate from that character's world.

Dialogue

124

In 1950, Henry Green gave a little talk on BBC radio about dialogue in fiction.* Green was obsessively concerned with the elimination of those vulgar spoors of presence whereby authors communicate themselves to readers: he never internalizes his characters' thoughts, hardly ever explains a character's motive, and avoids the authorial adverb, which so often helpfully flags a character's emotion to readers ("she said, grandiloquently"). Green argued that dialogue is the best way to communicate with one's readers, and that nothing kills "life" so much as "explanation." He imagined a husband and wife, long married, sitting at home one evening. At 9:30, the husband says that he is going across the road to the pub. Green noted that the wife's first response, "Will you be long?," could be rendered in scores of different ways ("Back soon?" "When will you be back?" "Off for long?" "How long will it be before you are back?"), each one capa-

---

Surviving: The Uncollected Writings of Henry Green, edited by Matthew Yorke (1992).

ble of a distinct resonance of meaning. The crucial thing, maintained Green, was not to hedge the dialogue with explanation, as in:

> "How soon d'you suppose they'll chuck you out?"
>
> Olga, as she asked her husband this question, wore the look of a wounded animal, her lips were curled back from the teeth in a grimace and the tone of voice she used betrayed all those years a woman can give by proxy to the sawdust, the mirrors and the stale smell of beer of public bars.

Green felt strongly that such kind of authorial "assistance" was overbearing, because in life we don't really know what people are like. "We certainly do not know what other people are thinking and feeling. How then can the novelist be so sure?"

Green, counseling against being overbearing, is laying down a fair amount of prescription himself, and we do not need to take his doctrine scripturally. Notice that when Green does his parody of explanation, he also falls into a deliberately breathy, second-rate style ("wore the look of a wounded animal"), whereas we can imagine something more continent, less offensive: "Olga knew what time he would come home, and in what state, stinking of beer and tobacco. Ten years of this, ten years." Fulsome explainers like George Eliot, Henry James, Marcel Proust, Virginia Woolf,

Philip Roth, and many others would all have to retire themselves in Green's universe.

However, his larger argument, that dialogue should be carrying multiple meanings, and that it should mean different things to different readers at the same time, is surely right. (It can carry several indeterminate meanings for the reader *and* still be "explained" by an author, I think, but this takes great tact.) Green offered an example of how he might proceed:

> He: I think I'll go across the way now for a drink.
> She: Will you be long?
> He: Why don't you come too?
> She: I don't think I will. Not tonight, I'm not sure, I may.
> He: Well, which is it to be?
> She: I needn't say now, need I? If I feel like it I'll come over later.

In this passage, notice that Green tries to answer one question with another, and that, very characteristically of Green's writing, the woman slides in hesitation—"Not tonight, I'm not sure, I may." She may be in several moods at once. As a result, the man's response, "Well, which is it to be?" becomes harder to read, too. Is he irritated, or just mildly resigned? Does he in fact want her to come to the pub at all, or was he just saying it in the hope that she would decline? The reader tends to plump for one reading, while being aware that multiple readings are also possible; we sew ourselves into the text, becoming highly invested in *our* version of events.

There is a very good example of Green's doctrine in action in V. S. Naipaul's great novel *A House for Mr Biswas*. Mr. Biswas has decided to build a house, but he only has a hundred dollars. He visits a black builder, Mr. Maclean (one of the few portraits in the novel of a black Trinidadian), and gingerly poses the question. What is beautifully done is that both men are dancing a little pas de deux of pride and shame; each is maintaining a fiction. Mr. Biswas wants Maclean to think he has enough money for a grand house; Maclean wants Biswas to think he is very busy, with lots of orders for work. And each sees through the other's fiction, of course.

Mr. Biswas begins by suggesting that they take the thing very slowly (that way, he can pay some money each month rather than place a huge sum down immediately). Ideally, Biswas would have Maclean take about a year to build the place:

> "We not bound and 'bliged to build the whole thing right away," Mr Biswas said. "Rome wasn't built in a day, you know."
>
> "So they say. But Rome get build. Anyway, as

soon as I get some time I going to come and we
could look at the site. You have a site?"

"Yes, yes, man. Have a site."

"Well, in about two-three days then."

He came early that afternoon, in hat, shoes and
an ironed shirt, and they went to look at the site.

At the site, Mr. Biswas announces that he wants
concrete pillars, plastered and smooth. Maclean
wants his cash:

"You think you could give me about a hundred and
fifty dollars just to start off with?"

Mr Biswas hesitated.

"You musn't think I want to meddle in your private affairs. I just wanting to know how much you
want to spend right away."

Mr Biswas walked away from Mr Maclean,
among the bushes on the damp site, the weeds and
the nettles. "About a hundred," he said. "But at the
end of the month I could give you a little bit more."

"A hundred."

"All right?"

"Yes, is all right. For a start."

They went through the weeds and over the leaf-
choked gutter to the narrow gravelly road.

"Every month we build a little," Mr Biswas said.
"Little by little."

"Yes, little by little."

The dance of pride is so delicately done. Biswas first couches his shame in a classical allusion, hoping to give it a bit of grandeur ("Rome wasn't built in a day, you know"), to which Maclean replies with a practical grunt: "So they say. But Rome get build," Naipaul subtly using Trinidadian patois—"But Rome get build"—to separate the two men and their social status. Mr. Biswas is aware of this social difference, too, because, when Maclean then asks if he has a site, he tries to close the gap by also using "black" patois: "Yes, yes, man. Have a site." (Whenever Biswas wants a bit of borrowed bravado, he employs the pally Caribbean word "man.") Maclean affects to be so busy that he cannot come for several days, and then arrives "early that afternoon."

And then it all begins again, over the question of money. Maclean is perfectly aware that Mr. Biswas is trying to save face, and flatters him with the absurd "You mustn't think I want to meddle in your private affairs." And relentlessly, Naipaul reminds the reader that the site itself is leaf-choked and weed-infested, that the whole thing is doomed from the start. (In this, he is a good deal more of an explainer and pointer than the very reticent Henry Green.)

125

And the same novel reminds us that Green is not necessarily right to assume that "dialogue is the best way for the novelist to communicate with his readers." As much can be communicated with no speech at all. It is Christmas, and Mr. Biswas, on a whim, decides to buy a hideously expensive doll's house for his daughter. He can't possibly afford it. He blows a month's wages on the gift. It is an episode of madness and bravado, of aspiration and longing and humiliation.

> He got off his bicycle and leaned it against the kerb. Before he had taken off his bicycle clips he was accosted by a heavy-lidded shopman who repeatedly sucked his teeth. The shopman offered Mr Biswas a cigarette and lit it for him. Words were exchanged. Then, with the shopman's arm around his shoulders, Mr Biswas disappeared into the shop. Not many minutes later Mr Biswas and the shopman reappeared. They were both smoking and excited. A boy came out of the shop partly hidden by the large doll's house he was carrying. The doll's house was placed on the handlebar of Mr Biswas's cycle and, with Mr Biswas on one side and the boy on the other, wheeled down the High Street.

Not a word of dialogue—indeed the opposite, the report of a dialogue we do not witness:

"Words were exchanged." Again, this is both funny and terribly painful, because of the way Naipaul writes it up. He resolutely refuses to describe the purchase itself. Instead, he describes the scene as if the author had set up a camera outside the shop. We watch the men smoke, we watch them go in, and a minute later we watch them come out, "smoking and excited." The scene is thus like something out of the silent movies, and almost begs to be run at double speed, as farce. Passive verbs are used, precisely because Biswas is a weak, comically gentle man who thinks he is asserting himself while he is in fact generally being acted upon: "was accosted by . . . the doll's house was placed on the handlebar . . . [was] wheeled down the High Street." Naipaul deliberately describes this event as if Mr. Biswas had nothing much to do with it, which is probably how Biswas self-forgivingly thinks of this moment. Most subtle is the decision not to represent the scene of purchase itself, the moment where money changes hands. This is the epicenter of shame for Mr. Biswas, and it is as if the narrative, knowing this, *is too embarrassed to represent this shame*. Naipaul is superbly aware of this, superbly in control. He knows that the sentence "Words were exchanged" is the pivot of the paragraph—because, of course, it is not *words* that are importantly exchanged but *money* that is crucially exchanged. And this is what cannot, must not, be described.

Several days later, the doll's house will be smashed to bits by Mr. Biswas's wife, because she thinks it unfair that their daughter got such a present while none of the other children that constitute Mr. Biswas's horribly extended family received anything.

Truth, Convention, Realism

Falsehood is so easy, truth so difficult.*

Here are two recent statements about literary realism, statements so typical of their age, so finely characteristic, so normative, that a realist novelist would have been proud to have imagined them into life. The first is by the novelist Rick Moody, writing in *Bookforum*:

> It's quaint to say so, but the realistic novel still needs a kick in the ass. The genre, with its epiphanies, its rising action, its predictable movement, its conventional humanisms, can still entertain and move us on occasion, but for me it's politically and philosophically dubious and often dull. Therefore, it needs a kick in the ass.

The second is by Patrick Giles, contributing to a long, raucous discussion about fiction, realism, and fictional credibility on a literary blog called

---

*George Eliot, *Adam Bede*.

The Elegant Variation: "And the notion that this [the realistic novel] is the supreme genre of the lit tradition is so laughable that I ain't even gonna indulge myself."

A style unites the two statements, a down-home relaxation of diction ("kick in the ass," "ain't even gonna"), which itself informs us about the writers' attitudes toward realism's own style: it is stuffy, correct, unprogressive, and the only way even to discuss it is to mock it with its stylistic opposite, the vernacular. Moody's three sentences efficiently compact the reigning assumptions. Realism is a "genre" (rather than, say, a central impulse in fiction-making); it is taken to be mere dead convention, and to be related to a certain kind of traditional plot, with predictable beginnings and endings; it deals in "round" characters, but softly and piously ("conventional humanisms"); it assumes that the world can be described, with a naively stable link between word and referent ("philosophically dubious"); and all this will tend toward a conservative or even oppressive politics ("politically . . . dubious").

127

Still, we know what Rick Moody means. Let's call this "novelism." We have all read many novels

in which the machinery of convention is so
rusted that nothing moves. Why, we say to ourselves, do people have to speak in quotation
marks? Why do they speak in scenes of dialogue? Why so much "conflict"? Why do people
come in and out of rooms, or put down drinks,
or play with their food while they are thinking
of something? Why do they always have affairs?
Why is there always an aged Holocaust survi-
vor somewhere in these books? And please,
whatever you do, don't introduce incest . . .

In a very witty essay written in 1935, Cyril
Connolly demanded that a whole family of conventions should be butchered—"all novels deal-
ing with more than one generation or with any
period before 1918 or with brilliant impoverished children in rectories," all novels set in
Hampshire, Sussex, Oxford, Cambridge, the
Essex coast, Wiltshire, Cornwall, Kensington,
Chelsea, Hampstead, Hyde Park, and Hammer-
smith.

> Many situations should be forbidden, all getting and
> losing of jobs, proposals of marriage, reception of
> love-letters by either sex . . . all allusion to illness or
> suicide (except insanity), all quotations, all mentions
> of genius, promise, writing, painting, sculpting, art,
> poetry, and the phrases "I like your stuff," "What's
> his stuff like?" "Damned good," "Let me make you

some coffee," all young men with ambition or young women with emotion, all remarks like "Darling, I've found the most wonderful cottage" (flat, castle), "Ask me any other time, dearest, only please—just this once—not now," "Love you—of course I love you" (don't love you)—and "It's not that, it's only that I feel so terribly tired."

Forbidden names: Hugo, Peter, Sebastian, Adrian, Ivor, Julian, Pamela, Chloe, Enid, Inez, Miranda, Joanna, Jill, Felicity, Phyllis.

Forbidden faces: all young men with curly hair or remarkable eyes, all gaunt haggard thinkers' faces, all faunlike characters, anybody over six feet, or with any distinction whatever, and all women with a nape to their neck (he loved the way her hair curled in the little hollow at the nape of her neck).*

Realism, for Moody and Giles, is like Connolly's opinion of a character named Miranda or Julian; it is just another convention reflecting the aspirations of petit bourgeois readers. Barthes argued that there is no "realistic" way to narrate the world. The nineteenth-century author's naive delusion that a word has a necessary and transparent link to its referent has been nullified. We move merely among different, compet-

---

*"More About the Modern Novel" in *The Condemned Playground: Essays 1927–1944* (1945).

ing genres of fiction-making, of which realism is just the most confused, and perhaps the most obtuse because the least self-conscious about its own procedures. Realism does not refer to reality; realism is not realistic. Realism, said Barthes, is a system of conventional codes, a grammar so ubiquitous that we do not notice the way it structures bourgeois storytelling.*

In practice, what Barthes means is that conventional novelists have pulled the wool over our eyes: a smooth wall of prose comes toward us, and we rather lazily gasp out loud: "How did it all come about?"—just as Flaubert wanted us to. We no longer bother to notice such elements of fiction as the convention that people speak within quotation marks ("'Nonsense,' he said, firmly"); that a character is briskly summarized in external description when he or she first enters a novel or story ("She was a shortish, broad-faced woman of about fifty, with rather poorly dyed hair"); that detail is carefully chosen and helpfully "telling" ("She noticed that his hands shook slightly as he poured the whisky"); that dynamic and habitual detail is conflated; that dramatic action is nicely broken up by characters' reflections ("Sitting quietly at the table, his head propped on one arm, he thought again

*See *S/Z* (1970).

about his father"); that characters change; that stories have endings; and so on. We are mired in novelism.

128

No one would deny that writing of this sort has indeed become a kind of invisible rule book, whereby we no longer notice its artificialities. One reason for this is economic. Commercial realism has cornered the market, has become the most powerful brand in fiction. We must expect that this brand will be economically reproduced, over and over again. That is why the complaint that realism is no more than a grammar or set of rules that obscures life is generally a better description of le Carré or P. D. James than it is of Flaubert or George Eliot or Isherwood: when a style decomposes, flattens itself down into a genre, then indeed it does become a set of mannerisms and often pretty lifeless techniques. The efficiency of the thriller genre takes just what it needs from the much less efficient Flaubert or Isherwood, and throws away what made those writers truly alive. And of course, the most economically privileged genre of this kind of largely lifeless "realism" is commercial cinema, through which most people nowadays receive their idea of what constitutes a "realistic" narrative.

129

Decomposition like this happens to any long-lived and successful style, surely; so the writer's—or critic's, or reader's—task is then to search for the irreducible, the superfluous, the margin of gratuity, the element in a style—in any style—which cannot be easily reproduced and reduced.

130

But rather than do that, Barthes and Moody and Giles and Willam Gass and many other opponents of fictive convention conflate different complaints. Here is Barthes in 1966: "The function of narrative is not to 'represent,' it is to constitute a spectacle still very enigmatic for us but in any case not of a mimetic order . . . 'What takes place' in the narrative is, from the referential (reality) point of view literally nothing; 'what happens' is language alone, the adventure of language, the unceasing celebration of its coming."* Now, to charge fiction with conven-

---

*From "Introduction to the Structural Analysis of Narratives" (1966). Quoted in Antoine Compagnon, *Literature, Theory, and Common Sense*, translated by Carol Cosman (2004). Notice that Barthes sounds very little different, in the end, from Plato, for whom mimesis was merely an imitation of an imitation. The real reason for the French obsession with the fraudulence of realism—and with fictional narrative in general—has

tionality is one thing; to move from this charge to the very skeptical conclusion that fictive convention can therefore never convey anything real, that narrative represents "literally nothing," is extreme. First, all fiction is conventional in one way or another, and if you reject a certain kind of realism for being conventional, you will also have to reject for the same reason surrealism, science fiction, self-reflexive postmodernism, novels with four different endings, and so on. Convention is everywhere, and triumphs like old age: once you have reached a certain seniority, you either die of it, or with it. One of the nice comedies of Cyril Connolly's essay is that by blacklisting every conceivable convention he effectively bans the writing of any fiction at all— "anybody over six feet, *or with any distinction whatever.*" Second, just because artifice and convention are involved in a literary style does not mean that realism (or any other narrative style) is so artificial and conventional that it is incapable of referring to reality. Narrative can be conventional without being a purely *arbitrary, nonreferential* technique like the form of a sonnet or the sentence with which Snoopy always

---

to do with the existence in French of the preterite, a past tense reserved exclusively for *writing* about the past, and not used in speech. French fiction, in other words, has its own, dedicated language of artifice, and thus must seem, to certain minds, unbearably "literary" and artificial.

begins his stories ("It was a dark and stormy night . . .").

131

Paul Valéry was hostile in a Barthes-like way to the claims of fictional narrative, and his example of an entirely arbitrary fictional premise was a sentence like: "The Marquise went out at five o'clock." Valéry felt, as William Gass did when discussing James's Mr. Cashmore, that this sentence is exchangeable with an infinite number of other possible sentences, and that this kind of provisionality robs narrative fiction of its necessity and its claim to probability. But as soon as I place a second sentence on the page—"That letter, received in the morning, had irritated the Marquise, and she was going to do something about it," say—the first sentence no longer looks quite as arbitrary or peremptory or merely formal. A system of relations and affiliations is beginning to quicken. And as Julien Gracq points out,* "Marquise" and "five o'clock" are not arbitrary at all, but full of limit and suggestion: a marquise is not an ordinary, interchangeable citizen, and five o'clock is still late afternoon while

---

*En lisant en écrivant (1980).

six is drinks time. So what is the Marquise going out for?

132

The point to make about convention is not that it is untruthful per se, but that it has a way of becoming, by repetition, steadily more and more conventional. Love becomes routine (and indeed Barthes once claimed that "I love you" is the most clichéd thing anyone can say), but falling in love is not nullified by this fact. Metaphors become dead through overuse, but it would be insane to charge metaphor itself with deadness. When the first caveman, shivering, said that he was as cold as ice, his interlocutor probably exclaimed: "That is pure genius!" (And after all, ice is cold.) Likewise, if someone were now to paint in the style of Rembrandt, he would be a third-rate copyist, not an original genius. These are the simplest arguments, and one should not have to make them, were it not for a persistent tendency among those hostile to verisimilitude to confuse convention with an inability to refer to anything truthful at all. Brigid Lowe* argues that the question of fiction's referentiality— does fiction make true statements about the

---

Victorian Fiction and the Insights of Sympathy (2007).

world?—is the wrong one, because fiction does not ask us to *believe* things (in a philosophical sense) but to *imagine* them (in an artistic sense): "Imagining the heat of the sun on your back is about as different an activity as can be from believing that tomorrow it will be sunny. One experience is all but sensual, the other wholly abstract. When we tell a story, although we may hope to teach a lesson, our primary objective is to produce an imaginative experience." She proposes that we restore the Greek rhetorical term "hypotyposis," which means to put something before our eyes, to bring it alive for us. (Somehow I don't think that "hypotyposis" will displace "realism" as the preferred term any time soon.)

133

Karl Ove Knausgaard has a productive way of thinking about the fatigue of convention. In the second volume of *My Struggle*, Knausgaard writes that, like many contemporary writers, he had lost faith in contemporary fiction. He would read the new novels, and they invariably struck him as false, artificial, too obviously "made up." This boring sameness, as he saw it, had to do with verisimilitude and its unchanging relation to the real: "verisimilitude and the distance it held to reality was constant." He came to the conclusion that fictional narration had no value, and instead turned to those forms where he could still find value and meaning: diaries and essays, "the types of literature that did not deal with narrative, that were not about anything, but just consisted of a voice, the voice of your own personality, a life, a face, a gaze you could meet."

The similarities with Roland Barthes's anti-realism are obvious, but the differences are powerful, too. The problem, Knausgaard implies, is not that there is no such thing as the real, or that artists shouldn't be concerned with the real, or that narration cannot possibly capture it. The problem is not even with the claims or ambitions of verisimilitude per se. The problem is with endlessly reproducing the same kind of verisimilitude, and the same fixed relation to the world it is describing. ("Fixed" in both senses: unchanging and somehow rigged or faked, *because* it is unchanging.)

Knausgaard has produced the creative work you might expect from a writer with these particular philosophical and aesthetic scruples. He has adjusted the lens, he has closed the gap between writing and the world; he shakes things up. He cares little about shapely narrative form; he floods his narratives with voice and personality—autobiography, essayistic interventions, opinions about art and music and philosophy; he avoids "obvious" fiction-making (dramatic scenes, domestic arguments, clever dialogue, punchy "conflict"); and he writes directly about the difficulty of writing truthful fiction in our age. But he is not an anti-realist; on the contrary, he is intensely interested in the real, in what writing *can* authentically disclose. He is tired of conventional verisimilitude—tired of novelism—not because he wants less of the real but because he wants more of it, differently produced. You could say he is a super-realist, the world's most fanatical realist.

134

The dilemma, for creative writers still interested in making things up, is that the consequences of Barthes's epistemological radicalism are ultimately self-defeating. If fictive language only falsifies reality, and is only about itself, then the logical response would be to atone for such falsity by ceasing to invent fictions, and to create, instead—well, to create perhaps, the body of work that Roland Barthes himself made, a beguiling mixture of criticism, theory, fragment, memoir, and commentary about the falsity of conventional fiction-making.

In practice, most postmodern novelists hedge

their bets. Postmodern novelists continue to make up fictions, but they want to do so on different terms, the most prominent being that they simultaneously acknowledge that they are making up those fictions. So the metafictional* or self-reflexive novel tends to have an atmosphere of confession, of knowing or ironic acknowledgment—admitting to, sometimes atoning for, often knowingly and joyfully delighting in the fact that it *is* a fiction. Of course, there are multiple ways of performing such acknowledgment. There is the story within the story, or the character with the same name as the author (Paul Auster likes to use both of these devices); the novel that is about the experience of reading the novel you hold in your hand (Italo Calvino's *If on a winter's night a traveler*); the novel that is being written by one of the characters you are reading about (Alejandro Zambra's *Ways of Going Home*, Ian McEwan's *Atonement*). There are books that offer the reader the chance to arrange the order in which they read them (Julio Cortázar's *Hopscotch*, Ali Smith's *How to Be Both*), or to choose between different endings (John Fowles's *The French Lieutenant's Woman*), or to ask that the reader construct a coherence—a story—that the

---

*One of the best guides to these terms is Linda Hutcheon's classic work, *A Poetics of Postmodernism* (1988).

fiction itself seems to refuse or obstruct (Claude Simon's *The Flanders Road*, Roberto Bolaño's *The Savage Detectives*).

135

Such writers reach back into the novelistic tradition, because one of the first great novels, *Don Quixote*, is a vibrant, funny, tender, and deeply serious fiction that is also a joyous commentary on the making of fiction, and indeed on the fictionality of reality. (In the second part of Cervantes's novel, the "real" Don Quixote, our beloved hero, must face down an imposter who claims that *he* is the real Don Quixote.) Perhaps most profound fictions—even ones we don't think of as experimental or avant-garde or postmodern—include or encode some acknowledgment of their own fictionality, or some kind of critique of the perils and obligations of fiction-making; that's a part of what makes them serious and profound. Serious artists like Cervantes are engrossed by the ways in which we go about constructing our realities, the fictions that we use to support and propel our often fantastic interior lives; so by implication (and often explicitly), they are interested in their own, analogous methods of such construction. I have in mind, for instance, the way that Shakespeare often reminds us of the staginess of the stage (in *King Lear*, when Gloucester thinks he is falling off a cliff, he is just dropping down onto the stage); the intrusive authorial narrators of many eighteenth- and nineteenth-century novels, who break in with advice and exegesis and thus disrupt the illusion, the flow, of novelistic artifice (Fielding, George Eliot, Gogol, Melville, Stendhal, Tolstoy); the many supposedly "conventional" novels, following Cervantes's model, that are about heroes and heroines who have been reading too much fiction (*Eugene Onegin*, *A Hero of Our Time*, *Notes from Underground*, *Madame Bovary*, *Niels Lyhne*, *A Confederacy of Dunces*, *The Fortress of Solitude*).

136

My own taste in postmodern art tends toward those works that simultaneously disrupt and validate our sense of reality, works that comment on story-making and which are, at the same time, intensely invested in the world we inhabit. These are almost magical instances of construction and deconstruction, of addition and subtraction. I have mentioned Saramago, Sebald, Spark, Philip Roth, Beckett, Lydia Davis, Alejandro Zambra. But take, as one final instance, Abbas Kiarostami's film, *Through the Olive Trees*.

As in everything he does, Kiarostami narrates a complex self-conscious tale with the utmost simplicity. An Iranian director is making a film, in rural northern Iran, and needs a leading man and woman. The young actor who is eventually selected turns out, in his ordinary life, to be actually in love with the woman who is playing opposite him. He has asked her to marry him, but she has refused because he has no house and is illiterate. On the film set, however, the couple must act as husband and wife. Kiarostami wrings the most tender comedy out of such small things as the woman's refusal to address the actor, on set, as "Mr. Hossein," as she would do if he were her husband. The actors have to do a scene in which the husband asks his wife where his socks are. They are not very good at it, and numerous takes ensue. Off the set, the young man, filled with ardor, assures the skeptical young woman that if they were really married he would actually know where his socks were.

The two young characters in *Through the Olive Trees* are utterly solid and realized; and, paradoxically, their solidity is not softened by Kiarostami's postmodern self-consciousness but magically enhanced by it. (I would happily forever watch the two of them rehearsing the scene about the socks.) Kiarostami's fascination with fictionality—his films often collapse the theatrical fourth wall—*emerges naturally from his great interest in the real*, as one might be very interested, say, in colors because one loved flowers, or in angels because one believed in God.

137

If we reexamine Aristotle's original formulation of mimesis, in the *Poetics*, we find that his definition is not about reference. History shows us, says Aristotle, "what Alcibiades did"; poetry—i.e., fictional narrative—shows us "the kind of thing that would happen" to Alcibiades. Hypothetical plausibility—probability—is the important and neglected idea here: probability involves the defense of the credible *imagination* against the incredible. This is surely why Aristotle writes that a convincing impossibility in mimesis is always preferable to an unconvincing possibility. The burden is instantly placed not on simple verisimilitude or reference (since Aristotle concedes that an artist may represent something that is physically impossible), but on mimetic *persuasion*: it is the artist's task to convince us that this could have happened. Internal consistency and plausibility then become more important than referential rectitude. And this task will of course involve much fictive artifice and not mere reportage.

So let us replace the always problematic word "realism" with the much more problematic word "truth" . . . Once we throw the term "realism" overboard, we can account for the ways in which, say, Kafka's *Metamorphosis* and Hamsun's *Hunger* and Beckett's *Endgame* are not representations of likely or typical human activity but are nevertheless harrowingly truthful texts. This, we say to ourselves, is what it would feel like to be outcast from one's family, like an insect (Kafka), or a young madman (Hamsun), or an aged parent kept in a bin and fed pap (Beckett). There is still nothing as terrifying in contemporary fiction, not even in the blood-bin of Cormac McCarthy or the sadistic eros of Dennis Cooper, as the moment when Knut Hamsun's narrator in *Hunger*, a starving young intellectual, puts his finger in his mouth and starts eating himself. None of us, I hope, has done this, or will ever want to. But Hamsun has made us share it, has made us feel it. Dr. Johnson, in his "Preface to Shakespeare," reminds us, "Imitations produce pain or pleasure, not because they are mistaken for realities, but because they bring realities to mind."

138

Convention itself, like metaphor itself, is not dead; but it is always dying. So the artist is always trying to outwit it. But in outwitting it, the artist is always establishing another dying convention. It is this paradox that explains the further, well-known literary-historical paradox, one we have witnessed through the course of this book, from Flaubert to Knausgaard, namely that poets and novelists repeatedly attack one kind of realism only to argue for their own kind of realism. It is summarized in Flaubert's remark about pornography: "Obscene books are immoral because untruthful. When reading them, one says, 'That's not the way things are.' Mind you, I detest realism, though I am claimed as one of its pontiffs." On the one hand, Flaubert wants nothing to do with the movement of "realism"; on the other, he deems certain books "untruthful" because they do not depict things as they are. (Chekhov used a similar formulation when watching an Ibsen play: "But Ibsen is no playwright . . . Ibsen just doesn't know life. In life it simply isn't like that.") Thomas Hardy argued that art wasn't realistic because art is "a disproportioning—(i.e. distorting, throwing out of proportion)—of realities, to show more clearly the features that matter in those realities, which, if merely copied or reported inventorially, might possibly be observed, but would more probably be overlooked. Hence 'realism' is not Art." Yet Hardy, of course, no less than Flaubert, strove to write novels and poems that show "the way things are." Who has written more beautifully or more truthfully than Hardy about rural communities, or about grief?

These writers rejected mere photographic fidelity, because art selects and shapes. But they revered truth and truthfulness.

Most major movements in literature in the last two centuries have invoked a desire to capture the "truth" of "life" (or "the way things are"), even as the definition of what is "realistic" changes (and of course even as what counts as "life" changes somewhat, too—but that *this* definition changes does not mean that there is no such thing as life). Woolf rightly complained that E. M. Forster, in *Aspects of the Novel*, was always invoking "life," and that it reflected a residual hearty Victorianism on Forster's part. Woolf properly argued that we judge fiction's success not just for its ability to evoke "life" but for its ability to delight us with more formal properties, like pattern and language:

> At this point perhaps the pertinacious pupil will demand: but what is this "life" that keeps on cropping up so mysteriously in books about fiction?

> Why is it absent in a pattern and present in a tea party? Why, if we get a keen and genuine pleasure from the pattern in the *Golden Bowl*, is it less valuable than the emotion which Trollope gives us when he describes a lady drinking tea in a parsonage? Surely the definition of life is too arbitrary and requires to be expanded? Why, again, should the final test of plot, character, story and the other ingredients of a novel lie in their power to imitate life? Why should a real chair be better than an imaginary elephant?*

But on the other hand, she also complained that "life escapes" from the fiction of Arnold Bennett and his Edwardian generation, and that "perhaps without life nothing else is worth while."† She praised Joyce for coming closer to "life," and sweeping away a host of dead conventions. Alain Robbe-Grillet, in his book *Pour un nouveau roman*, rightly says, "All writers believe they are realists. None ever calls himself abstract, illusionistic, chimerical, fantastic." But, he goes on to say, if all these writers are mustered under the same flag, it is not because they agree about what realism is; it is because they want to use

---

*"Is Fiction an Art?" (1927).
†"Modern Fiction" (1922).

their different idea of realism to tear each other apart.

If we add to these examples the invocations of "Nature" beloved of neoclassical critics, the overwhelmingly strong Aristotelian tradition with its distinction between probability and the improbably marvelous (accepted by Cervantes, Fielding, Richardson, Dr. Johnson), the claim made by Wordsworth and Coleridge that the poems in *Lyrical Ballads* offer "a natural delineation of human passions, human characters, and human incidents," and so on, we are likely to think of the desire to be truthful about life—the desire to produce art that accurately sees "the way things are"—as, if not a universal literary motive, then the broad central language of the novel and drama: what James in *What Maisie Knew* calls "the firm ground of fiction, through which indeed there curled the blue river of truth." "Realism" and the technical or philosophical squabbles it has engendered seem like a school of bright red herrings.

139

And in our own reading lives, every day, we come across that blue river of truth, curling somewhere; we encounter scenes and moments and perfectly placed words in fiction and poetry, in film and drama, which strike us with their truth, which move and sustain us, which shake habit's house to its foundations: King Lear asking forgiveness of Cordelia; Lady Macbeth hissing at her husband during the banquet; Pierre almost executed by French soldiers in *War and Peace*; the tattered band of survivors wandering the city streets in Saramago's *Blindness*; Dorothea Brooke in Rome, realizing that she has married a man whose soul is dead; Gregor Samsa, being pushed back into his room by his own, horrified father; Kirilov, in *The Possessed*, writing his suicide note, with the awful Peter Verkhovensky by his side, suddenly and ridiculously bursting out: "Wait! I want to draw a face with the tongue out on the top . . . I want to tell them off!" Or the beautiful little scene in *Persuasion* when Anne Elliot, kneeling on the floor, and keen to get a heavy two-year-old boy off her back, is suddenly relieved of the burden by the man she secretly loves, Captain Wentworth:

> Someone was taking him from her, though he had bent down her head so much, that his little sturdy hands were unfastened from around her neck, and he was resolutely borne away, before she knew that Captain Wentworth had done it.
>
> Her sensations on the discovery made her perfectly speechless. She could not even thank him. She

could only hang over little Charles, with most disordered feelings.

Or the last chapter of Willa Cather's *Death Comes
for the Archbishop*, some of the most exquisite
pages ever written in American fiction.* Father
Latour has returned to die in Santa Fé, near his
cathedral: "In New Mexico he always awoke a
young man; not until he rose and began to shave
did he realize that he was growing older. His
first consciousness was a sense of the light dry
wind blowing in through the windows, with the
fragrance of hot sun and sage-brush and sweet
clover; a wind that made one's body feel light
and one's heart cry 'To-day, to-day,' like a child's."
Lying in his bed, he thinks about his old life in
France, about his new life in the New World,
about the architect, Molny, who built his
Romanesque cathedral in Santa Fé, and about
death. He is lucid and calm:

> He observed also that there was no longer any per-
> spective in his memories. He remembered his win-
> ters with his cousins on the Mediterranean when he
> was a little boy, his student days in the Holy City,
> as clearly as he remembered the arrival of M. Molny

---

*Pages surely influenced by Chekhov's story about a dying bishop, "The
Bishop," and an influence, in turn, on Marilynne Robinson's *Gilead*.

and the building of his Cathedral. He was soon to have done with calendared time, and it had already ceased to count for him. He sat in the middle of his own consciousness; none of his former states of mind were lost or outgrown. They were all within reach of his hand, and all comprehensible.

Sometimes, when Magdalena or Bernard came in and asked him a question, it took him several seconds to bring himself back to the present. He could see they thought his mind was failing; but it was only extraordinarily active in some other part of the great picture of his life—some part of which they knew nothing.

140

Realism, seen broadly as truthfulness to the way things are, cannot be mere verisimilitude, cannot be mere lifelikeness, or lifesameness, but what I must call *lifeness*: life on the page, life brought to different life by the highest artistry. And it cannot be a genre; instead, it makes other forms of fiction seem like genres. For realism of this kind—lifeness—is the origin. It teaches everyone else; it schools its own truants: it is what allows magical realism, hysterical realism, fantasy, science fiction, even thrillers, to exist. All the greatest realists, from Austen to Alice Munro, are at the same time great formalists.

But this will be unceasingly difficult: for the writer has to act as if the available novelistic methods are continually about to turn into mere convention and so has to try to outwit that inevitable aging. Chekhov's challenge—"Ibsen just doesn't know life. In life it simply isn't like that"—is as radical now as it was a century ago, because forms must continually be broken. The true writer, that free servant of life, is one who must always be acting as if life were a category beyond anything the novel had yet grasped; as if life itself were always on the verge of becoming conventional.

Bibliography

Novels, short stories, and narratives referred to or quoted from in this book are listed below. In the interest of evoking a sense of historical passage and context, I have ordered them by first date of publication in their original language. Translators have been credited in those cases in which I have quoted at any length from one particular translation.

Miguel de Cervantes, *Don Quixote* (1605 and 1615)

The Bible, King James Version (1611)

Daniel Defoe, *Robinson Crusoe* (1719)

Henry Fielding, *Joseph Andrews* (1742), *Tom Jones* (1749)

Denis Diderot, *Rameau's Nephew* (written in the 1760s, published in 1784)

Jane Austen, *Pride and Prejudice* (1813), *Emma* (1816), *Persuasion* (1818)

Alexander Pushkin, *Eugene Onegin* (1823–31)

Stendhal, *The Red and the Black* (1830, translated by Margaret Shaw)

Honoré de Balzac, *La Peau de chagrin* (1831), *Splendeurs et misères des courtisanes* (1839–47)

Stendhal, *The Charterhouse of Parma* (1839)

Mikhail Lermontov, *A Hero of Our Time* (1840)

Charlotte Brontë, *Jane Eyre* (1847)

William Makepeace Thackeray, *Vanity Fair* (1848)

Charles Dickens, *David Copperfield* (1850)

Gustave Flaubert, *Madame Bovary* (1857, translated by Geoffrey Wall)

George Eliot, *Adam Bede* (1859)

Charles Dickens, *Great Expectations* (1861)

Fyodor Dostoevsky, *Notes from Underground* (1864), *Crime and Punishment* (1866)

Gustave Flaubert, *Sentimental Education* (1869, translated by Robert Baldick)

Leo Tolstoy, *War and Peace* (1869, translated by Louise and Aylmer Maude)

George Eliot, *Middlemarch* (1871–72)

Thomas Hardy, *Far from the Madding Crowd* (1874)

Leo Tolstoy, *Anna Karenina* (1877)

Fyodor Dostoevsky, *The Brothers Karamazov* (1880)

Jens Peter Jacobsen, *Niels Lyhne* (1880)

Henry James, *The Portrait of a Lady* (1881)

Thomas Hardy, *The Mayor of Casterbridge* (1886)

Leo Tolstoy, *The Death of Ivan Ilyich* (1886)

Guy de Maupassant, *Pierre and Jean* (1888)

Knut Hamsun, *Hunger* (1890)

Thomas Hardy, *Tess of the D'Urbervilles* (1891)

Anton Chekhov, "Ward 6" (1892), "Rothschild's Fiddle" (1894)

Theodor Fontane, *Effi Briest* (1894)

Stephen Crane, *The Red Badge of Courage* (1895)

Henry James, *What Maisie Knew* (1897)

Anton Chekhov, "The Lady with the Little Dog" (1899)

Theodore Dreiser, *Sister Carrie* (1900)

Thomas Mann, *Buddenbrooks* (1901)

Anton Chekhov, "The Bishop" (1902)

Joseph Conrad, *Heart of Darkness* (1902)

Beatrix Potter, *The Tailor of Gloucester* (1903)

Rainer Maria Rilke, *The Notebooks of Malte Laurids Brigge* (1910, translated by Stephen Mitchell)

Leo Tolstoy, *Hadji Murad* (1912)

Marcel Proust, *Remembrance of Things Past* (1913–27, translated by C. K. Scott Moncrieff and Terence Kilmartin)

James Joyce, *Dubliners* (1914)

Franz Kafka, *The Metamorphosis* (1915)

D. H. Lawrence, *The Rainbow* (1915)

James Joyce, *A Portrait of the Artist as a Young Man* (1916)

D. H. Lawrence, *Sea and Sardinia* (1921)

James Joyce, *Ulysses* (1922)

Katherine Mansfield, *The Garden Party and Other Stories* (1922)

Sinclair Lewis, *Babbitt* (1922)

Italo Svevo, *Confessions of Zeno* (1923)

Thomas Mann, *The Magic Mountain* (1924)

Willa Cather, *Death Comes for the Archbishop* (1927)

Virginia Woolf, *To the Lighthouse* (1927)

Isaac Babel, "My First Fee" (1928)

William Faulkner, *As I Lay Dying* (1930)

Virginia Woolf, *The Waves* (1931)

Louis-Ferdinand Céline, *Journey to the End of the Night* (1932)

Joseph Roth, *The Radetzky March* (1932)

Christopher Isherwood, *Goodbye to Berlin* (1939)

Robert McCloskey, *Make Way for Ducklings* (1941)

Henry Green, *Loving* (1945)

Evelyn Waugh, *Brideshead Revisited* (1945)

Vladimir Nabokov, "First Love" (1948)

Cesare Pavese, *The Moon and the Bonfire* (1950)

Ralph Ellison, *Invisible Man* (1952)

Vladimir Nabokov, *Lolita* (1955)

Saul Bellow, *Seize the Day* (1956)

Vladimir Nabokov, *Pnin* (1957)

Claude Simon, *The Flanders Road* (1960)

V. S. Naipaul, *A House for Mr Biswas* (1961)

Muriel Spark, *The Prime of Miss Jean Brodie* (1961)

Julio Cortázar, *Hopscotch* (1963)

John Updike, *Of the Farm* (1965)

John Williams, *Stoner* (1965)

Thomas Pynchon, *The Crying of Lot 49* (1966)

Frederick Exley, *A Fan's Notes* (1968)

B. S. Johnson, *Christie Malry's Own Double-Entry* (1973)

Italo Calvino, *If on a writer's night a traveler* (1979)

Thomas Bernhard, *Wittgenstein's Nephew* (1982)

José Saramago, *The Year of the Death of Ricardo Reis* (1984)
Cormac McCarthy, *Blood Meridian* (1985)
Philip Roth, *The Counterlife* (1986)
Kazuo Ishiguro, *The Remains of the Day* (1989)
Norman Rush, *Mating* (1991)
Cormac McCarthy, *All the Pretty Horses* (1992)
W. G. Sebald, *The Emigrants* (1992)
Philip Roth, *Sabbath's Theater* (1995)
Penelope Fitzgerald, *The Blue Flower* (1995)
Roberto Bolaño, *The Savage Detectives* (1998)
Ian McEwan, *Atonement* (2001)
J. M. Coetzee, *Elizabeth Costello* (2003)
Norman Rush, *Mortals* (2003)
Jonathan Lethem, *The Fortress of Solitude* (2003)
Marilynne Robinson, *Gilead* (2004)
David Foster Wallace, *Oblivion: Stories* (2004)
Thomas Pynchon, *Against the Day* (2006)
John Updike, *Terrorist* (2006)
Lydia Davis, *Collected Stories* (2009)
Karl Ove Knausgaard, *My Struggle* (2009–2011)
Alice Munro, *Selected Stories* (2011)
Teju Cole, *Open City* (2011)
Alejandro Zambra, *Ways of Going Home* (2011)
Denis Johnson, *Train Dreams* (2012)
Elena Ferrante, *My Brilliant Friend* (2012)
Jenny Offill, *Dept. of Speculation* (2014)
Ali Smith, *How to Be Both* (2014)

Index